Words, science
and learning

DEVELOPING SCIENCE AND TECHNOLOGY EDUCATION

Series Editor: Brian Woolnough
Department of Educational Studies, University of Oxford

Current titles:

John Eggleston: *Teaching Design and Technology*
Clive Sutton: *Words, Science and Learning*

Titles in preparation include:

David Layton: *Technology's Challenge to Science Education*
Michael Poole: *Beliefs and Values in Science and Technology Education*
Keith Postlethwaite: *Teaching Science to Pupils with Special Educational Needs*
Michael Reiss: *Science Education for a Pluralist Society*
Jon Scaife and Jerry Wellington: *Information Technology in Science and Technology Education*
Joan Solomon: *Teaching Science, Technology and Society*

Words, science and learning

CLIVE SUTTON

Open University Press
Buckingham · Philadelphia

Open University Press
Celtic Court
22 Ballmoor
Buckingham
MK18 1XW

and
1900 Frost Road, Suite 101
Bristol, PA 19007, USA

First Published 1992

*A catalogue record of this book is available from
the British Library*

*Library of Congress Cataloging-in-Publication
Data*

Sutton, C. R. (Clive Remer), 1936–
    Words, science, and learning/Clive Sutton.
        p.   cm. – (Science and technology
        education)
    Includes index.
    ISBN 0–335–09957–2
    ISBN 0–335–09956–4 (pbk.)
    1. Lexicology.   2. Semantics.
    3. Science – Language.
    I. Title.   II. Series.
    P326.S87   1992
    501′.4 – dc20   91–45905
                                            CIP

Typeset by Type Study, Scarborough
Printed in Great Britain by
St Edmundsbury Press, Bury St Edmunds,
Suffolk

You can hardly imagine how I am struggling to exert my poetical ideas just now for the discovery of analogies and remote figures respecting the earth, sun, and all sorts of things – for I think that is the true way (corrected by judgment) to work out a discovery.

Michael Faraday (1845) in a letter to
C. F. Schoenbein

Mere words?

Acids, atoms and **accelerations**
Cycles, circuits, ceramics and **cells**
Decomposition!

Energy, enzymes, embryos and **ecosystems**

Fuels and **flames** and **focal lengths**

Habitat, Hypothesis

James Prescott Joule

Minerals, metals and **metabolism**
Pressure, purity and **plastics**
Photo . . . synthesis

Sperms and **spectra, sensors** and **sense organs**
Tests and **tectonics**
Volts, vibrations and **velocities**
Wavelengths and **watts**

Some words from our national curriculum in science.
What did people have in mind when they brought these words into scientific use, and how do we make sense of them now?

Contents

Series editor's preface

It may seem surprising that after three decades of curriculum innovation, and with the increasing provision of centralised national curriculum, that it is felt necessary to produce a series of books which encourage teachers and curriculum developers to continue to rethink how science and technology should be taught in schools. But teaching can never be merely the 'delivery' of someone else's 'given' curriculum. It is essentially a personal and professional business in which lively, thinking, enthusiastic teachers continue to analyse their own activities and mediate the curriculum framework to their students. If teachers ever cease to be critical of what they are doing then their teaching, and their students' learning, will become sterile.

There are still important questions which need to be addressed, questions which remain fundamental but the answers to which may vary according to the social conditions and educational priorities at a particular time.

What is the justification for teaching science and technology in our schools? For educational or vocational reasons? Providing science and technology for all, for future educated citizens, or to provide adequately prepared and motivated students to fulfil the industrial needs of the country? Will the same type of curriculum satisfactorily meet both needs or do we need a differentiated curriculum? In the past it has too readily been assumed that one type of science will meet all needs.

What should be the nature of science and technology in schools? It will need to develop both the methods and the content of the subject, the way a scientist or engineer works and the appropriate knowledge and understanding, but what is the relationship between the two? How does the student's explicit knowledge relate to investigational skill, how important is the student's tacit knowledge? In the past the holistic nature of scientific activity and the importance of affective factors such as commitment and enjoyment have been seriously undervalued in relation to the student's success.

And, of particular concern to this series, what is the relationship between science and technology? In some countries the scientific nature of technology and the technological aspects of science make the subjects a natural continuum. In others the curriculum structures have separated the two leaving the teachers to develop appropriate links. Underlying this series is the belief that science and technology have an important interdependence and thus many of the books will be appropriate to teachers of both science and technology.

Clive Sutton's book makes an important and timely challenge to the accepted orthodoxy with regard to the dominance of practical work in science. He stresses the centrality of language in scientific thinking, and in particular the use, and abuse, of metaphor. It is one of those rare books which provide a quantum leap in our thinking about science and technology teaching, and gives a new meaning to what it means to be 'doing science'.

We hope that this book, and the series as a whole, will help many teachers to develop their science and technological education in ways that are both satisfying to themselves and stimulating to their students.

Brian E. Woolnough

CHAPTER 1

In praise of words

Words can have a power and influence quite out of proportion to their triviality as mere marks on paper or vibrations in the air. When circumstances are right they can excite people's minds and move their imaginations, in science as in any other area of human activity. This is true even of single words, such as **energy** or **embryo**, but it is even more true of 'words' in the sense of extended statements which elicit meaning in the prepared mind. I think for example of the tremendous understatement made by Watson and Crick in 1953 when they set down their thoughts about the form of a DNA molecule – a double helix held together by attractions along the molecular chain. For readers who understood the problem, the effect of these lines must have been electrifying:[1]

> **It has not escaped our notice that the specific pairing we have postulated immediately suggests a possible copying mechanism for the genetic material.**

Words are amongst the tools of the job in the research institute and in the classroom, as people work towards new thoughts, but how exactly do they act on human minds? How have they done so in the growth of scientific ideas? That is the main theme of this book, and from it I hope to trace some consequences for science in schools, where it seems to me that words and word-based activities are accorded too low a status as compared with practical work at the bench. More than a decade ago some teachers of English set out a case for 'language for learning' or 'language across the curriculum'. They were concerned that in the

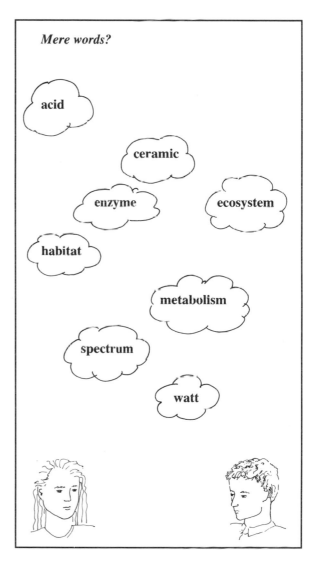

Mere words?

acid

ceramic

enzyme

ecosystem

habitat

metabolism

spectrum

watt

routines of a secondary school some pupils can become too passive in their learning, with insufficient demand on them to re-formulate ideas in their own words. Such arguments are still powerful today, and they constitute one of the influences on me in writing this book. A second and more powerful strand of thought, however, has emerged from developments in the history and sociology of science, which make it important to think again about the role of language in science. These developments are part of a changing conception of the nature of science. By taking them into account I believe we might resolve the otherwise conflicting demands on busy science teachers – to manage practical work well, but also to organise a range of other language-centred activities.

Practical work essential?

Practical work has a special importance for science teachers because of our confident belief that reliable knowledge must be based in direct experience. Along with this confidence, we inherit from our forebears a fear of 'mere words', and a hostility towards wordiness, the basis of which must be understood in any re-appraisal. I shall explore its origins (in Chapter 4) and show how the scientific community has developed very distinctive beliefs about language, and its relationship to knowledge.

Here I simply note that some distrust of verbalism is quite justified. After all, what are words, without experience and imagery to bring them to life? All too readily they are empty words, quite apart from the possibility that they are lies. We recoil from the idea that anyone should learn from books alone, or by dictation and rote recitation, without experience and evidence. We rejoice in the contrast that science can offer. Come and see this, handle this, and try it for yourself . . .

Surely we are right to believe that learners should feel for themselves what a magnetic force is like or what happens when you stretch a spring? That is the first of three common kinds of practical work (listed in the panel below), and anything I write in this book will assume its importance – giving the tangible experience which brings ideas to life. A second kind is skill-orientated; for example we want pupils to practise for themselves how to use a thermometer or how to wire a circuit, and to gain feelings of competence as they do so. Lastly there is a third sort of 'learning by doing' which many teachers claim to be important. They argue that when it comes to understanding what is meant by a 'scientific investigation' there is no substitute for trying one yourself. The new national curriculum in England and Wales sets an expectation that every child in the land will regularly be involved in such investigations.[2]

I do not wish to deny the importance of first-

Three kinds of practical work*

 (i) **experiencing a phenomenon,**

 (ii) **exercising a measurement skill or some other useful procedure from the craftsmanship of science,**

(iii) **investigating in the sense of carrying out a small enquiry in the scientific tradition.**

* See Brian Woolnough and Terry Allsop (1985) *Practical Work in Science*, Cambridge University Press. The national curriculum for England and Wales, introduced in 1989 and revised in 1991, specifies an entitlement for pupils to be involved in planning as well as doing investigations. This goes some way towards ensuring that the practical activities will be adequately embedded in a process of grappling with scientific ideas, but more generally there remains a problem of connecting practical work with the discussion and appreciation of ideas. For a possible solution to this problem see Chapter 9, and the description of **WORD WORK** as the core of a science lesson.

hand experience at all, but an exaggerated confidence in the value of handling 'things' as opposed to playing with 'mere words' can amount almost to an idolatry of the bench. Practical activities can become so prominent that they leave little space for learners to reflect on ideas, or for teachers to organise the means for them to do so. Practical work is in danger of having a higher status than careful discussion of the meaning of ideas. Until recently teaching schemes gave very detailed guidance on practical work, but much less on how to plan thinking, talking and writing activities. These other lesson components are fortunately receiving more attention in current schemes of work, but they may not be used effectively if learners or their teachers continue to act as if the practical work were the source of knowledge, with language just a descriptive commentary. Hence the need for this enquiry into what language does, and how words work in science. I shall be arguing for a more explicit recognition that practical experience can never 'speak for itself', but that the words we use are necessary interpretive instruments of understanding.

Thoughts into words and words into thoughts

Ideas influence the production of words – but how? When a scientist tries to express a new idea and later when a young learner tries to grapple with that same idea, what happens? What happened for Boyle, or Faraday, or Darwin wrestling with new thoughts? What happens for Angela or Sanjay or any of the other youngsters who are working their way through school now? This is the first question I have in mind. It is often asked about pupils' beliefs – where do they get their ideas from? – but I shall be asking it about scientists in the first instance, especially in the early chapters.

A second focus is the point of reception of words. How do they manage to elicit thought in someone else? What are the circumstances in which words become meaningful, and how does that sense of meaning grow and change over time?

Linking these two aspects of thought and word, there are some convictions at the back of my mind which I shall try to substantiate:

- The words chosen by any speaker or writer help to crystallise his or her thoughts, and subsequently steer that person's perceptions
- Sometimes – but not always – one person's words elicit in somebody else a corresponding shift of perception
- Thoughts of this kind are invariably accompanied by some aspect of feeling, which is no less important than their intellectual effect

Words and persuasion

The linkage of thought and feeling is particularly important. It seems to me that words do not just inform, they persuade. I shall need to devote quite a lot of space to how they do so because in science we have emphasised their descriptive functions, and played down their persuasive power. Some aspects of it have been explicitly rejected in science, as we can see in the following quotation from 1667, about the aspirations of members of the Royal Society to avoid rhetoric and use a simple descriptive language:

> **On avoiding flowery persuasive language:**
> Thomas Sprat in his *History of the Royal Society of London* (1667) comments on the style of reports written by the Fellows;
>
> **Their purpose is . . . to make faithful Records of all the works of Nature . . . And to accomplish this they have indeavour'd to separate the knowledge of nature from the colours of Rhetorick, the devices of Fancy, or the delightful deceit of Fables.**

Unfortunately, the distinction between 'faithful records' and 'fanciful rhetoric' is not as simple as Mr Sprat thought, and 'recording what happened' is often better thought of as a persuasive re-description. If only for that reason, the persuasive role of language deserves more serious attention in the classroom. A teacher has to deal in persuasion, in both its intellectual and its emotional aspects.

When you are concerned with someone's grasp of ideas you are in effect persuading them into new points of view, new ways of seeing things, new patterns of interpreting and understanding the world. If you are coaching youngsters in personal competence, then it is persuasion of a slightly different kind, well expressed by a headmaster of the last century:

> . . . getting at the heart and mind of the learner so that he comes to value learning and to believe it possible in his own case.[3]

This book, therefore, will explore the persuasive role of words as well as their thought-crystallising and thought-provoking power. It will question some very long-established assumptions about language in science, with a view to forming a modern account that is relevant to teaching today. It will be about the role that words have played in the growth of scientific ideas, as well as their role in the growth of a learner's understanding. It will be mainly a *theoretical* enquiry, trying to identify principles rather than to offer a lot of detailed practical (or impractical!) advice, and it must be exploratory rather than definitive. Drawing on themes which have been stated elsewhere, I shall try to refine partially formed theories and to offer a tentative opinion about their consequences. 'Opinion', like 'persuasion' has seemed a word not entirely decent in polite scientific company, yet we are not far from realising anew that to ask pupils to express their opinions is not just an incidental part of knowing them, and in the classroom it need not be seen as just some wild activity indulged in by teachers of 'soft' subjects. I hope that what I write will bear on the practical question of how to offer effective science education for citizens. It is likely also to touch on such long-standing problems as the alleged coldness of science and its perceived distance from the human concerns of many adolescents.

Thinking with a pencil

Trying to plan what should be included, I have found myself repeatedly 'thinking with a pencil', abandoning the word processor to sketch on real paper the shape of what I hope to say. Pencil is almost as easy to edit as words on a screen, and a pencil as an aid to thought may well be superior to a computer, more like an extension of one's hand, and so of oneself. Does such a drafting and thinking process have a place in school science? What are pencils for, anyway? In the busy routines of a science lesson they have usually seemed to be just devices for recording something, and much less obviously instruments for sorting out ideas. I notice however that Michael Faraday and Charles Darwin used their pens very effectively for thinking and re-drafting, as well as for reporting, and today's learners are entitled to experience both uses. I want to clarify the rationale for each, because of the dominance of the long-established school tradition that pencils are mainly for reporting.

The National Curriculum implies that a greater proportion of the available time will be allocated for pupils to formulate what they think, to say how an investigation should be planned, what they estimate might happen in the proposed experiments, and what is their favoured explanation for what is going on. Could the pencil ever come to rival the Bunsen burner as one of the items most characteristic of a science lesson? Could the text-editing software or the stock of poster paper for reports by committees become as obvious in the laboratories of tomorrow as the balance or the circuit board is today? Certainly this book will point in that direction. At present it is not the pencil, but the Bunsen burner and the circuit board which seem most characteristic. Much can come from handling them, but it seems increasingly clear that practical experience of itself does not bring about learning until it is animated by ideas, and these ideas are carried in words. For new experience to be properly linked in with a learner's thought, more attention will have to be paid to words and what is done with them. That includes the pupil's own words, the teacher's words, and the words of those who first created the ideas. So in the next chapter I will start by looking at the choice of words at some important points in the growth of scientific ideas.

Notes

1 Watson, J. D. and Crick, F. H. C. (1953) 'A structure for deoxyribose nucleic acid', *Nature,* **171**, 737–8. See also Francis Crick's autobiographical account: *What Mad Pursuit*, Weidenfeld and Nicolson, 1988. Crick remarks (p. 66) that some readers saw the quoted statement as 'coy', and he claims that it was put in as a compromise between the desire to discuss the genetic implications and fear of going too far in doing so.

2 National Curriculum: *Science: Programmes of Study and Attainment Targets*, HMSO, 1989. In relation to the experience of investigation, see especially Attainment Target 1 – 'Exploration of Science'. In the first revision of these targets (1991) it has been retitled simply as 'Scientific Investigation'. For a comprehensive discussion of all aspects of practical work see Woolnough, B. (ed.) (1990) *Practical Science*, Open University Press.

3 Quotation from Edward Thring, Head of Uppingham School from 1853 to 1887.

A prelude to Chapter 2   **HOW DID WE COME TO TALK LIKE THIS?**

Where did the following words and expressions come from? Many of them are in effect 'fossils' of old thoughts. What were those thoughts, that led someone to choose these particular words for the purposes they first served in science? In most cases they continue to serve similar purposes today. Try to find clues by matching the words to your existing knowledge of language. Then if necessary consult a dictionary written on historical principles and find out about earlier meanings. Further information about some of these expressions is given in the text of Chapters 2 and 3.

Conductors and **insulators** in the physics of electricity and also of hot and cold things

Harnessing the energy of a waterfall, or measuring the **horsepower** of an engine

Latent heat

Cell (in biology and in physics)

Test-tube in chemistry

Niche (in ecology)

Messenger RNA in cell chemistry. Who thought of it in this way, and when? How does it connect with other imagery of information transfer used in the discussion of nucleic acids?

Chapters and **topics**. Why are the divisions of books called chapters, and how did a 'topic' come to be so called?

A **parasite** in your intestine. How is the modern biological meaning of the word 'parasite' related to its earlier meanings? Has the exact biological meaning avoided the pejorative feeling that attaches to its other uses? A word which has a somewhat similar history to 'Parasite' is 'Satellite', and it will serve as a worked example. After Galileo saw the moons of Jupiter through his telescope, Kepler called them 'Satellites' from their appearance as 'attendants' to Jupiter. In Latin *satelles* described an attendant on some more important person. We now use the word in many contexts in a manner close to its early meaning, e.g. when we speak of 'satellite towns' to a large centre like London, or of eastern European countries as former satellites of the Soviet Union, but we have also given it a new derived meaning by extension from that of Kepler when we speak of 'weather satellites' and its metaphorical origins are substantially dormant.

CHAPTER 2

Fossils of old thoughts

One way to appreciate how words are involved in transformations of thought is to pause in our *use* of scientific language and consider its origins. That is a bit like stopping to look afresh at a landscape one has known for years without understanding its geological composition and history. You gradually start to see how its modern form reveals past events. A similar change of stance is possible for the language. Although we often take it for granted and use words without any knowledge of where they came from, a closer inspection reveals much evidence of the activities and thoughts of previous generations. Once we start to view scientific expression with the eye of an archaeologist or a palaeontologist we can find clues to those thoughts, and glimpse the process by which new ideas were articulated.

Scientific language is a record of the work of *people*, and even if we are mainly interested in the objectified outcomes of their work, this human aspect is not lightly to be ignored where our purposes are educational. Why for example do the names of certain bits of chemical equipment have such a French ring? Why do we have pipettes (little pipes?) and burettes (little bures?). With them you find a reliable 'titre' (a measure of how much of the significant stuff is really there), and this process we now describe with a new verb: 'to titrate' something. The efforts of French chemists and technicians are commemorated almost by accident in the way that the international community has taken up their vocabulary.

The British probably took up these words not only from a professed internationalism in their science, but also because there was no easy way to translate them into less Latinate alternatives. Anglo-Saxon words for measuring out liquids (pulling pints and drawing draughts) do not seem quite up to the precision demanded in the drop-by-drop matching of one liquid to another. The best we could probably manage would be 'dripper' or 'dropper' for the equipment, and it is easy to understand how the French terms had more appeal. They survived in English as well as in French, as part of a whole new craft called 'volumetric analysis'. Histories of chemistry suggest that it was Joseph Louis Gay-Lussac (1778–1850) who established this craft and that it served initially to find the 'titre' or assay-value of silver. The word titre as a description of the fineness or truly reliable content of precious metal connects with 'title' as in 'reliable title to property', or 'title deeds'.

When he developed the 'burette' as an instrument for such assay, Gay-Lussac must have adapted some pre-existing item of equipment from the kitchen or the vestry or the vineyard, but he also adapted a pre-existing word, and started a new branch of talking. Earlier assays had involved melting the metal, but his idea was that the real silver in a silver sample could be counted off against measured amounts of a wet reagent. It was an exciting idea to his contemporaries, and it is this thought which is now fossilised in our word **titration**. Once people got hold of the idea of drop-by-drop matching of solutions to find the amount of substance in one of them, it was generalised and applied to all sorts of different

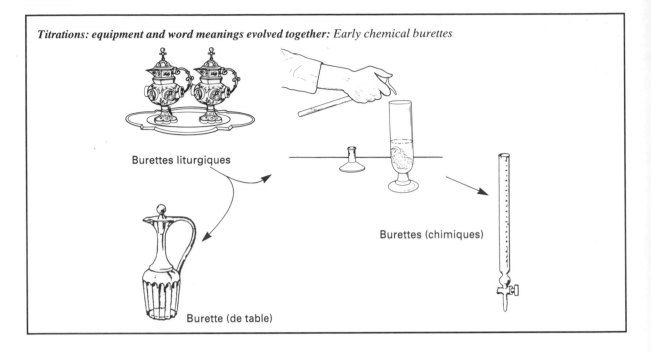

Titrations: equipment and word meanings evolved together: Early chemical burettes

Burettes liturgiques

Burettes (chimiques)

Burette (de table)

problems. Hence the need for words to describe it, and by the 1860s, 'titration' was a taken-for-granted part of a chemist's thought and speech. Discussion of the experimental techniques blended in with theoretical talk about the reacting 'equivalents' of substances, and the system sustained whole laboratories of chemists for over a hundred years.

Volumetric analysis is less important now, and one day these words may fade from use. (Chemical 'equivalent' has already almost gone.) In retrospect the period begins to look like an episode in the growth, change and decay of language. I shall return later to the value of recognising how very flexibly mutable and impermanent language is – and that includes scientific language.

A word from the yeast

Staying for a moment with the European dimension to our science, here is a much more important and enduring word, where we can follow idea-formation in the word itself: the word is **enzyme**. Textbooks often refer to its invention from Greek *en – zymos* (something in the leaven, in the yeast).

First it was formed in German as *Enzym*, and then taken into English as *enzyme*. Its emotional impact does not always come through in those accounts, perhaps because words in science are supposed to be uncontaminated with emotion. However, some German chemists in the middle and later decades of the last century were confident that there was something in the juices of the yeast, not the living yeast itself, that caused the fermentation of sugars. Ultimately some of them had the satisfaction of being right, and they squeezed it out and labelled it. Later it turned out to be more than one substance, and the word had to be generalised to mean any one of them or others like them, and another new branch of scientific conversation was launched. Well, not so much 'launched' perhaps, as consolidated. The selection and successful use of the word 'enzyme' was part of a larger theoretical movement that resulted in the demystification of what had previously been called 'protoplasm', and in the possibility of discussing what went on in the interior of cells as a series of ordinary chemical reactions. It led to our modern concepts of metabolism and metabolic pathways. Incidentally, some of the derivatives of 'enzyme', such as 'enzymosis', have died out while others (e.g. 'enzymic reaction') have remained in use. All these words have been part of a change in how we theorise about living cells, and in them we see that when there is something difficult to interpret, words in a sense *are* theories. When someone finds it necessary to make a new word, or to use an old one in a different way, they are trying out some framework of understanding, some way of thinking about the topic in hand, some way of seeing what is going on. When others hear and repeat such words they too are engaging with that way of theorising.

Words connected with electric charge

One example of this process of word and theory interaction is in the choice and enjoyment of the word **jar** in the days of public excitement about the first electrical machines. The **Leyden Jar** became popular after experiments by Pieter van Musschenbroek in the town of Leyden in 1745, and it was one of the first devices to accumulate (or condense or collect or intensify) the mysterious 'electric charge'. Friction machines caused the appearance of this charge. It seemed possible to pass it from object to object and along threads or chains or wires, and the 'jars' were evidently a means of collecting it if you thought of it as either some kind of loose material, or some kind of fluid.

The word **charge** itself was borrowed from other uses – as in charging a gun with gunpowder – and it was a word which helped to firm up the idea that there might be something real and measurable – the 'quantity of electricity', with a limit to how much of it you could put into or onto something. To capture it might well require a jar-shaped container, and trials with water or lead shot or mercury inside such jars also made sense as they might absorb the otherwise elusive stuff or help to 'condense' it, lest it should waft away.

Later, however, it appeared that no jar-shape was needed at all, and that two layers of metal separated by glass or even air achieved similar effects. Nevertheless, the community went on talking about the 'capacity' of such devices for

---

Public interest in theory and spectacle: An advertisement from 'The Times' newspaper, September 28 1804

Flattered by the unbounded approbation of a numerous and brilliant Audience, and at the particular request of several Persons who were present at the last lecture, Mr HARDIE is induced to repeat his interesting LECTURE upon his new Hypothesis of the ELECTRIC and GALVANIC FLUIDS, at the LARGE THEATRE, LYCEUM, TO-MORROW, when the surprising effects of the Galvanic Influence on the muscular and nervous system will be evinced . . . As the whole of the theatre upon this occasion will be illuminated by the combustion of hydro-carbonic gas which renders the use of candles, lamps &c totally unnecessary, the Public will have an unusual opportunity of scientific gratification.

Earlier ways of talking about electrical charge

Earlier ways of trying to describe and understand electrical phenomena included the notions of 'electrical effluvia' around and emanating from the rubbed amber or glass, and of 'electrical virtue' which could be communicated from one object to another by touch or along threads.

'Effluvium' suggests something quasi-material, whereas 'electrical virtue' sounds (to us) more like a quality or property than an actual stuff. However, as the threads along which this electrical virtue could be communicated grew longer and longer, and were strung out across galleries, barns and gardens, the principal investigator concerned (Stephen Gray, around 1729) found himself using such phrases as 'to carry the electric virtue' or to 'convey' it. It is almost as if some stuff were gradually materialising in his mind.

Eventually 'electrical virtue' was supplanted completely by 'electrical charge' – finite, measurable, and with fewer metaphysical overtones.

For a full case study of the development of such ideas see Case Study 8 by D. Roller and D. H. Roller in the *Harvard Case Studies in Experimental Science*, eds J. B. Conant. and L. K. Nash (Harvard University Press, 1957).

charge because the idea of 'electrical matter' was successful in other ways. Until very recently these devices were still called 'condensers' for electricity – a small fossil of thoughts that lived two centuries ago.

Notwithstanding problems that arose then and since with two-fluid and one-fluid theories about electricity, the common vocabulary is still based on that imagery. We still speak of 'currents' 'flowing' in 'conductors', i.e. the conduits for that flow.

Words connected with heat

Our vocabulary about hot and cold things also shows the influence of thoughts and theories of long ago, even though we say that such theories have been abandoned. We claim now that 'heat' is just a sort of internal agitation or tremor – an opinion which did not appeal to Joseph Black (1728–99), the Scotsman who did much to establish quantitative methods for the measurement of heat.[1]

Accounts of Black's work suggest that he was cautious of explanatory theory at all, but it seems to me that in those days there was such a growing belief in the 'capacity' of different materials for heat that the language was firmly set in the direction of a fluid theory. Less reticent thinkers, experimenters and writers found it very helpful to imagine heat as another of these 'very subtle' fluids which could flow in and out of things. They gave it various names (matter of heat, igneous fluid, caloric), which we have now dropped, but the idea is still preserved in our everyday language and our scientific language, in expressions such as **heat flow, conduction, heat sink** and **thermal capacity**.

If we value science as sets of interpretive ideas[2], then it is worth attending to these phrases, so that teachers and learners can feel the thought behind them. In one sense they are just fossils, but my metaphor breaks down because they are not quite as dead as the ammonites in the limestone cliff. They can be re-activated, re-vived, re-vitalised, to provoke one's mind just as they provoked the minds of people when they were first used.

Words for little things

Consider the word **molecule** – rather a dead-looking word if ever there was one. It is standard practice in British schools to try to teach about atoms and molecules or other particles as reasonable speculations to account for melting, evaporation, diffusion, etc. Researchers aver, however, that this effort is not as successful as we hope[3]. What is involved in re-activating such a word? If we do not want it to be just a label for some object that people are told to believe in, how can we make it once again into a lively speculation, with implications that the pupils' minds will explore for weeks to come? – more time perhaps, more speech by pupils and less by teachers, more skill in helping them to identify with characters in a role play, new strategies in marking their written work? Such approaches will be considered in later chapters, so here let me just come back to dwelling upon the word itself. When the word 'molecule' was first used it must have been quite clear that it meant a 'little lump', very very 'minuscule'. To get any feeling for that we may have to compare it with other diminutives for 'icle' things – animalcules as the little animals that Leeuwenhoek thought he saw with the microscope, 'particles' as little parts, and 'icicles' as little icethings. Then we start to wonder: 'How -icle? How -cule? What sort of lump?'

I hope that I am starting to answer one of the questions posed in Chapter 1, about thoughts and words. At least in some topics, words give the best clues we have to the thoughts on which the science was built.

Doubt and variability in the choice of words

Instead of tracing old thoughts by their remnants in present-day language, it is sometimes worth going back to what the innovators themselves said at points of uncertainty. In the adjacent panel, for example, we see Lavoisier struggling with whether or not to believe in the material reality of a heat-fluid, and what to call it. 'Can we really account for changes of state', he says, 'without

Antoine Lavoisier debates with himself how to explain the nature of heat and its effects in causing changes of state. From the Traité Élémentaire de Chimie (1789). English translation by Robert Kerr. (Original typestyle)

The fame may be affirmed of all bodies in nature : They are either folid or liquid, or in the ftate of elaftic aëriform vapour, according to the proportion which takes place between the attractive force inherent in their particles, and the repulfive power of the heat acting upon thefe ; or, what amounts to the fame thing, in proportion to the degree of heat to which they are expofed.

It is difficult to comprehend thefe phenomena, without admitting them as the effects of a real and material fubftance, or very fubtile fluid, which, infinuating itfelf between the particles of bodies, feparates them from each other ; and, even allowing the exiftence of this fluid to be hypothetical, we fhall fee in the fequel, that it explains the phenomena of nature in a very fatisfactory manner.

This fubftance, whatever it is, being the caufe of heat, or, in other words, the fenfation which we call *warmth* being caufed by the accumulation of this fubftance, we cannot, in ftrict language, diftinguifh it by the term *heat ;* becaufe the fame name would then very improperly exprefs both caufe and effect. For this reafon, in the memoir which I publifhed in 1777 *, I gave it the names of *igneous fluid* and *matter of heat :* And, fince that time, in the work † publifhed by Mr de Morveau, Mr Berthollet, Mr de Fourcroy, and myfelf, upon the reformation of chemical nomenclature, we thought it neceffary to banifh all periphraftic expreffions, which both lengthen phyfical language, and render it more tedious and lefs diftinct, and which even frequently does not convey fufficiently juft ideas of the fubject intended. Wherefore, we have diftinguifhed the caufe of heat, or that exquifitely elaftic fluid which produces it, by the term of *caloric.* Befides, that this expreffion fulfils our object in the fyftem which we have adopted, it poffeffes this farther advantage, that it accords with every fpecies of opinion, fince, ftrictly fpeaking, we are not obliged to fuppofe this to be a real fubftance ;

---

thinking of them as the effects of some real substance which can insinuate itself amongst the particles of a solid and collapse its structure? It seems that way, and I and my friends have decided to call the substance **caloric**, rather than some of the longer possible names. Of course, strictly speaking you don't have to believe it is real . . .'

Elastic aeriform vapours

Another important phase in the evolution of scientific thought is seen in the first sentence of the quotation from Lavoisier, where he refers to everything being able to exist either as solid or liquid, or as 'elastic aeriform vapour'. This very descriptive term is well worth reviving in modern science teaching because the elasticity, squeezability or springiness of gases can be experienced by pupils very easily.

All through the 1600s and 1700s the existence of a third state of matter was being clarified. 'Air' was seen to be something rather than nothing, and people realised that there were different 'airs'. Gradually ways were devised to trap and collect them, and they were called elastic aeriform vapours for a long time. Jan Baptist van Helmont (1577–1644) had chosen the word **gas**, from the Greek word *chaos* (using the aspirated 'g' of his own language to stand for the chi of the Greek) for what he saw as the spirit or essence of things – chaotic in its wild tendency to escape, for example on heating. After the improvement of bottling methods to catch and study such things, his word gained general acceptance in preference to 'airs', and it may well have helped the kinetic interpretation of evaporation as a chaotic movement of the component bits.

Chemical names

Lavoisier understood very clearly that control of language is involved when you are trying to sort out and establish new ideas. In the main part of his work on names of chemical substances he rejected all names that referred to their appearance (e.g. 'sugar of lead', 'butter of arsenic'). He believed that their appearance was not the most important feature. What mattered was what a substance was composed of, so he insisted that names like *oxyde d'argent* or *sulphure de fer* (oxide of silver, sulphide of iron) would be much better. Up to that time it was not obvious that appearance was less important, nor even that weight was important. The new system of naming actually helped people to attend to the known or supposed components of a substance. The chemical balance for weighing them grew in importance correspondingly.

Does it matter?

Is it important to attend to changes in language as a part of teaching? So far I have chosen examples where I believe that insight into the changes could help a modern learner to understand the interplay of words, ideas and experimental evidence. In other cases the origins of ways of speaking have been left behind so far that we can safely stick to the accepted literal meanings of a word, and not bother about its origins. That is my answer to those who ask me whether it matters to know the origins of words, technical terms, and ways of speaking. Sometimes it does make a difference, and in many other cases it does not (unless it be by altering your whole attitude to language). As language changes, novel figurative uses of words are gradually literalised and then you can operate with them just as if they had no past. You can use them simply as labels for the things or ideas to which they attach. For example, it would be difficult to argue that a person's ability to use a 'tele-phone' effectively is improved by reflecting on the origins of the word as 'distant-hearing' device. In France I can buy *essence* at the petrol station and think of it just as the stuff in the tank, or in the kitchen I might add 'essence of vanilla' to a cake, without reflecting that these substances have been obtained as distillates, and that early distillers thought they were somehow liberating the 'essence' or 'spirit' of what they heated.

The more familiar a word is, the more fossilised, dead or dormant it becomes, and the more difficult it can be to re-activate so that we see its earlier uses as an instrument of new thought. Perhaps that is justification enough for sticking to a present day literal meaning. Consider the word **tested**. Its literal meanings are either in connection with 'fair tests' and experiments, or with exams and mark sheets, and we might as well just use it without enquiring too closely into its antecedents. For interest, however, long ago *testa* in Latin was a 'small pot'. In one of its later appropriations, botanists took it over to describe the hard casing of a seed. Many centuries ago it had also suffered another twist when some jokers evidently saw a person's head or skull as a pot, and that route is thought to have led to the words for head in modern Italian (*testa*) and modern French (*tête*). In alchemy and metallurgy a little clay pot for the assay of gold was also a 'testa', and so 'tested gold' came to mean gold that had survived that particular ordeal. A more obviously figurative adaptation then extended this into the active parts of the verb 'to test', and gave us our modern meanings.

I will end this chapter with a more borderline case, where knowledge of the language may or may not make a difference. On the face of it I can set up the equipment for electroplating quite effectively, and talk of **anodes** and **cathodes**, and even of **ions** in the solution without knowing anything of the struggles that Michael Faraday had in 1833–4 to decide how to express his ideas about this topic. He asked William Whewell, later master of Trinity College Cambridge, what words would be most helpful, and part of their correspondence is available for visitors to see in the Wren Library of the college. Whewell drew on his mastery of Greek to favour 'anode and cathode' (the way up and the way down) for what Faraday was trying to express, rather than 'eisode and exode' (the way in and the way out), and certainly rather 'oriode and occiode' or 'east-ode and west-ode' which came from Faraday's thoughts about electricity and the earth's magnetism. Faraday had tried 'electrobeid' ('electrical goer') for whatever was migrating in the solution and Whewell suggested simply 'ion' to allow 'cation' at the cathode and 'anion' at the anode. (See pages 46 and 48 for a discussion of how the new words form a cluster.)

Many people must have carried out commercially useful electroplating, or scientific investigations into electrolysis, without ever knowing this little history. On the other hand, to savour the meaning of 'electrolyte' as a substance at least capable of being loosened and split in this way does seem important to working on them with any understanding.

It is true, I think, that one can get away with literal language, especially where the purpose is to teach an immediate practical competence rather than a more long-term insight. Since both are important goals in today's schools I take heart from how a Chief Inspector of Schools (J. G. Fitch) put it in 1880:

> **To become acquainted with words in their full significance is to know much about the things they represent and about the thoughts which other people have had.**

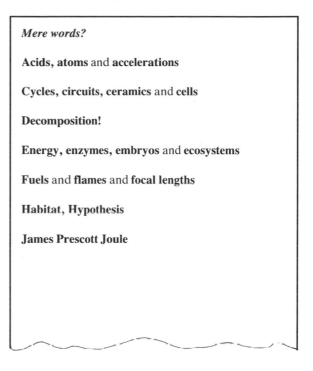

Mere words?

Acids, atoms and **accelerations**

Cycles, circuits, ceramics and **cells**

Decomposition!

Energy, enzymes, embryos and **ecosystems**

Fuels and **flames** and **focal lengths**

Habitat, Hypothesis

James Prescott Joule

Notes

1 Joseph Black's work: See Douglas McKie and Neils H. de V. Heathcote (1935) *The Discovery* [sic] *of Specific and Latent Heats*, Edward Arnold. The approach which Black and others worked out united in one system an understanding of such diverse phenomena as the slowness of melting of the highland snows in spring, the large amounts of heat needed to generate steam in James Watt's engines, and the problems of cooling whisky stills. Using it, people came to speak easily about the varying 'capacity' of different materials for heat, and also about the hidden heat which was evidently retained in liquids and vapours, having been taken up as they gained their fluidity.

The word 'discovery' used in the title of the above book is itself a fossil of an old thought about what scientists are doing – 'dis-covering' or uncovering what is simply 'there' to be uncovered. This word hardly acknowledges the contribution that the scientist makes to formulating the concepts, or the role of language in that formulation. Later chapters will explore why 'discovery' is not such an easy word to accept nowadays (see Chapter 11). Even in 1935 it might have been possible to call the book *The Invention of Specific and Latent Heats*, and today it might better be called *The Construction of the Ideas of Specific and Latent Heats*.

2 Science as sets of interpretive ideas: I should of course add that ideas in science are not just any old ideas, but ones which have supportive evidence from practical test. We are therefore justified in giving prominence to practical experience for those who learn. On the other hand a great deal of effort has gone into presenting the evidence and relatively little into helping the learners to enter imaginatively into a particular thought system for themselves and to understand why anyone should have wanted or needed it. We have hardly any well-proven techniques for assisting them in that way.

3 Adolescents' understanding of 'particle' in the context of a kinetic theory of matter: See Brook, A., Briggs, H. and Driver, R. (1984) *Aspects of Secondary Students' Understanding of the Particulate Nature of Matter*, Leeds University Centre for Studies in Science and Mathematics Education.

CHAPTER 3

Figuring things out with words

A second way to appreciate the role of words in the formation of new ideas is to focus on their non-literal uses, and see what happens to them in that situation. This chapter will be entirely about that problem, and it will draw on an extensive literature about metaphor in science which is briefly surveyed in the notes at the end of the chapter.

Expressing a new thought often involves putting words together that would not normally be linked. For example, millions of people have experienced successive nights of winter frost followed by a clouding over of the sky and a realisation that it is suddenly less cold. Someone, sometime, made sense of this situation by speaking of a **blanket of cloud** over the land. Other people, recognising the aptness of the image, have accepted and used the phrase ever since.

What happens to words when they are treated in this way, and how does it help us in the process of 'figuring out' what is going on? How did it help Michael Faraday, trying to make sense of the effects of a magnet, to start talking of a **magnetic field**? More recently, how did it help an eleven year old, beginning to understand a Bunsen burner, to describe it as 'a sort of **gas candle**'? These are not ordinary, literal, uses of words; there is figurative quality in them, a metaphorical usage if you like, but I prefer the general term 'figurative language' because it is more obviously something to do with trying out a new way of understanding. For a fuller insight into the role of words in science we need to recognise the functions of such language in our thought.

Hearing afresh the 'blanket of cloud'

The more unexpected a new phrasing is, the greater its effect becomes in provoking the mind into action. After long familiarity the effect wears off, and otherwise strange expressions may be accepted unquestioningly. That is already partly true of 'blanket of cloud', but with a little effort we can revive the novelty and hear it as it might have sounded on first use.

Certainly the words 'blanket' and 'cloud' cannot always have been associated, so what could anyone have had in mind? Clearly the cloud is *not* made of wool, but it *does* keep the warmth in, and satisfaction with that thought might be enough to sustain our continued involvement with the expression. We could explore it further, and for the scientifically curious there are similarities in the way a cloud and a blanket achieve their effects: by trapping air, by interrupting upward circulatory currents, and by reflecting radiant heat back downwards. The relative importance of each of these is probably *not* the same for a cloud and a woollen blanket. By throwing these words together both the generator of the phrase and its later recipients gain a means of understanding the cloud and of thinking about the experience of the cold evenings and the warmer ones. The two ideas of blanket and cloud stand together and tease one's mind. Although the main effect is that we see the cloud differently, we also modify slightly our meaning of the word blanket. It is no longer just a label for some manufactured item from Bradford,

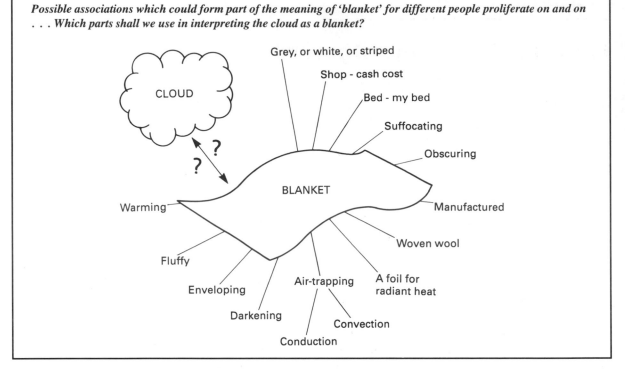

Possible associations which could form part of the meaning of 'blanket' for different people proliferate on and on . . . Which parts shall we use in interpreting the cloud as a blanket?

but a more generalised idea – something to enclose you, retaining warmth (whatever that is!). Perhaps we could have useful household 'blankets' which are not cloth at all but just some other means to stop heat escaping? Certainly we can now have a verb 'to blanket': the clouds blanket the land. That is one thing that figuring does to words; it shifts their meaning and prepares the way for new variants and derivatives.

This two-way effect is a feature of a theory of how metaphors work which I will describe later – the interactive or tensional theory. Nothing is quite explicit in the relationship of old and new meanings, but the hearer and the generator of the phrase explore what was said, not exactly for what was stated, but for what was *implied*.

Some people find it worrying that there is no limit to the possible implications. A cloud also keeps a lot of the sunlight *out*, as would throwing a blanket over your head, and some might see the phrase in that way, but its appeal probably lies mainly in its thermal message, or perhaps in its totality ('blanket coverage'). Probably we scan the

various aspects of the idea and take some seriously while rejecting others. For example, we do not think anyone is suggesting that clouds are made in Bradford, or indeed that they are manufactured at all. There is no warp and weft to a cloud, but on the other hand there *is* a fluffiness. A cloud would not suffocate you, but a cloud could hide you. And so on . . . Points of positive and negative connection will occur almost without one realising it.

The teasing relationship is strongest in the simple metaphor 'blanket of cloud', but you could also express the idea in a more limited and controlled way as a simile, 'Clouds are like a blanket'. You could also elaborate it into a model, 'Clouds considered as blankets: consequences for a quantitative study of heat retention'.

Metaphor, simile, model: all three are devices for figuring out what is happening, and for gaining new insights. Scientists require their models to have the added feature of generating explicit testable predictions, and therefore they make a point of elaborating them. Nevertheless these models have their origins in simpler figurations.

Another reason why I prefer to write about figuration or figurative speech is that the other terms elicit too many knowing winks. 'Oh, metaphors, that's English – fancy speech for poets' or 'Oh, you mean analogies; I had a good one for teaching electric current but . . .' or even 'The trouble with models is that my lot confuse the model with the real thing.' These reactions do not do justice to the intellectual importance of the topic. Figurative language[1] is *not* a private possession of those with degrees in English Literature. It is a major mental tool for anyone thinking anew, and that includes scientists working on new topics and school pupils who are learning scientific ideas. It consists in using language to extend language, of drawing on what is familiar and using it to interpret something else. In a culture which possesses blankets, the particular interpretive scheme which I have discussed could occur over and over again, with people drawing upon words and imagery from the more familiar situation to interpret the less familiar one.

What do you mean, 'computer virus'?

At the risk of repetition let us take a more recent example, where the sources of the figurative expression would *not* have been available to earlier generations: why are people talking and writing about **computer viruses**? I feel my mind pulled in several different directions by this phrase, and to explore them will assist a further reflection on the role of the startling metaphor in science, in communication and in learning. There is certainly heuristic potential in throwing these two words together. The phrase stops me, provokes me, and invites me to wonder what its author had in mind. Implications begin to elaborate themselves, and everything I know about biological viruses and computer programs is brought to bear on finding and appraising the connections.

> We are thinking of something 'infective'? Self-replicating? Small but powerful? Dangerous? Biological viruses have an entry point, and some autonomy when 'inside', but they depend on the internal processes of their host. So, it seems, do these 'software bugs'. Suddenly I realise that 'bug' was an earlier metaphor used by programmers as they searched in semi-affectionate exasperation for the parts of their program which were interrupting its smooth operation. There seems no end to the implications provoked by just two words! But bug to virus is a shorter leap than program to virus.

As in the previous example, the implications do not just flow one way.

> A program is information about how to do something. 'One purl, two plain' is a program which can generate row upon row of knitting in the sleeve of my new sweater. These software 'viruses' are really programmatic information which generates row upon row of unwanted transcript on the computer disc. Does that mean that biological viruses are programs too? Well, yes, we see the nucleic acids as a code which can initiate synthesis of proteins, and even – godammit – of more nucleic acids. That's how they reproduce themselves. My conscious understanding of the original virus is starting to alter in response to the metaphor, and not just my understanding of the computer what-not.
>
> O.K. I give in! I can't help it now. I see the software intruder *as a virus* and my concept of what a virus is has been enriched in the process of my being won over to this point of view.

These extended ideas about computer software on the one hand and biology on the other are so powerful that I wonder if they helped to motivate a desire to create computer viruses, and guided the process of doing so. Language may have guided invention.

A scientist's restraint

The feeling of 'giving in' to the imagery, of being taken over by it, and all too rapidly persuaded into a new viewpoint, is one about which scientists are justifiably cautious. Figures of speech can be so persuasive that we need some way of checking their usefulness. A politician or journalist speaks of countries 'falling like dominoes' under the influence of a neighbouring great power; we understand the point made and find it hard to escape the image, but is it a valid image? Is there really any evidence for the 'domino theory'?

Within science itself, it may be graphic to think of 'messenger' chemicals carrying 'transcripts' of 'genetic information' to parts of a cell, and of 'translation' of one chemical 'code' into another, but all this needs to be checked out against evidence, and for that purpose, in science, the first products of figuration are usually subjected to a critical review in which they have to be spelled out in sufficient detail to allow them to be testable, and then experimental evidence is marshalled.

As I feel myself heir to the language traditions of science, I can therefore give a quite different account of my response to **computer virus**:

> Computer virus? What is being said here? Surely a virus is something in biology isn't it? So what's this talk about viruses in computers? Oh, I see, it's some sort of analogy. The things get inside your computer and take over its systems and mess up its mechanisms – you mean *like* a virus in a cell. Some of them even reproduce themselves – *like* a virus does. I can see it might be a useful comparison in some ways, a useful analogy. We'd better be careful though; after all a virus is a virus, organic, biological, and we are really talking about software and computer discs. Analogies always break down, and they can be terribly misleading, especially for youngsters who confuse the analogy with the real thing . . . And anyway, isn't it too emotive to call something a virus? They scare people; people think of them as subversive, infiltrating, usurping, CIA and KGB-ish. Really, we could do with a more neutral term altogether to describe these whatever they are – these transferrable self-activating mini-programs.

Notable features of this reaction include (i) unease in the face of vivid language, (ii) a desire to explain away its functions as either *decorative* (it is not essential; there will be plainer ways of saying the same thing), or *didactic* (it is just an aid to explaining) and (iii) a scientist's preference for terms with few emotional connotations – the same inclination which prompts a scientist to write 'subcutaneous' instead of 'under the skin'. It is a reaction in which I do engage with the interpretive value of the phrase, but only in an extremely guarded way – seeking out the points of comparison item by item.

Interaction or point-by-point comparison?

My two responses to 'computer virus' illustrate respectively an interactive or tensional theory of metaphor, and a comparative one. The latter is widely held, and it is associated with the opinion that words have fixed meanings as labels for what they describe. Therefore in a metaphor all you can do is to compare the two parts and see how they resemble or differ from each other.

The interactive theory on the other hand is associated with the opinion that language is fluid, that it forms part of our systems for deciding what it is we see and what we know about it, as well as how to describe it, i.e. language is an interpretive system rather than just a labelling or descriptive system. On this view a metaphor brings into tension two previously disparate ideas and invites you to see one in terms of the other. This way of thinking about metaphoricity was developed by I. A. Richards (1936) and Max Black (1962). It also permeates Donald Schon's book (1963) about the more general problem of the origins of new ideas. (As he describes it, there is an evolution of ideas by displacement of old concepts from one situation to another.)[2]

A key feature of the interactive theory is the *indefiniteness in the meaning of existing words*, and therefore the unlimited number of implications which might be explored in the metaphor. This notion of indefinite, uncircumscribable, meaning contrasts starkly with attempts in science to tie down the meaning of words with greater and greater precision and to make them mean one thing and one thing only – definable and fixed.

About my second response, the cautious or sceptical one, I feel sad because it seems to degrade the metaphor in its original richness and make it the subject of a laboured and pedantic analysis. In the live metaphor the thoughts co-exist and continue to provoke insight, rather than allowing themselves to be spelled out in a list. I have similar feelings about the way in which narrative metaphors, i.e. parables, are sometimes converted into very contrived allegories. Like any other kind of figurative speech, a parable is attempting to develop a new understanding of something – often something which is rather difficult to comprehend. The 'message' of the parable however is inexplicit. C. H. Dodd[3] described a parable as:

> **a metaphor or simile drawn from nature or common life, arresting the hearer by its vividness and strangeness, and leaving the mind in sufficient doubt about its precise application to tease it into active thought.**

He considered the much-studied parables of Jesus, such as 'A certain man went down from Jerusalem to Jericho . . .' or 'A certain man had two sons . . .' and argued convincingly that in their original spoken form most of them presented one single main point of focus, the details of the story not being intended to have independent significance, but only included to heighten the vividness of the account.

Subsequently, several of those otherwise provocative stories have been converted into elaborate allegories by people who wanted to use them for a particular didactic purpose. For example, in the Parable of The Sower, the stony ground and the thistles among which some of the corn fell are given specific meanings. This allegorisation makes the whole story rather laboured and to my mind it is not a good way to teach, with the conclusions all ready-made for the learner. However, the process of trying to spell out the detail is quite like my cautious response to 'computer virus', and I accept that explicitness is often needed in science, e.g. when a scientific model is being used as a guide to designing experiments.

The relationships between some of the different kinds of figuration might be represented as follows, where vertical arrows show an increasing explicitness and elaboration.

Simile	**Metaphor**	**Parable**
		(narrative metaphor)
↓	↓	↓
Analogy	**Model**	**Allegory**

The loss of the teasing effect

Much-used figurative expressions gradually lose their mentally-teasing qualities and become literalised or accepted as having ordinary non-metaphorical meanings in their new context. For example, we speak of modern warships 'sailing' away from port and take this to mean that they departed; we give no thought to whether or not they had sails. If we hear that passengers who escaped a car crash were 'petrified' we understand that they were very much afraid and perhaps so gripped by fear that they were incapable of action on their own behalf. We accept what has become a nearly-literal word for extreme fear, though with a little effort we could recover the original figuration: they were 'petrified' with fear, i.e. 'turned to stone' or immobilised by it.

Commonly this loss of metaphorical power is itself described figuratively, as the fading or dying of a live metaphor. However if 'sailed' is a dead metaphor, then 'petrified' for frightened is not quite so dead, and so within a modern understanding of how novel language affects the mind it would be better to distinguish *active* and *inactive* metaphors, or we could speak of the latter as *dormant* (sleeping).[4] In education we could then describe one part of a teacher's work as reactivating dormant metaphors, and exercising professional judgement about when it would be useful to do so. Teachers of a whimsical inclination could think of teaching as an encounter of dormant minds with dormant words for the re-animation of both. However, many seemingly dormant minds are probably just resting.

Specialist scientific language is full of words and expressions in various stages of fading, dying, inactivation or dormancy. **Hydro-gen** was once actively understood as the stuff which could beget water or make water (*hydro-gène* in French) or even as the 'stuff of water' (*Wasserstoff* in German), but partly by intention and partly by neglect in long years of taken-for-granted use the word is now just a label for a certain flammable gas in a balloon or a bottle. The choice of the word **cell** by the early microscopists to make sense of what they saw as an array of compartments once gave it a lively connection with the monks' cells in a monastery or the parts of a honeycomb. Later, however, the word became just a literal label for a biological unit. Incidentally it has much changed in meaning in this century, to become a dynamic chemical system. So much for the idea that science works with terms of fixed meaning!

Still moderately active is the biological word **niche**. From being a cavity in a rock, a safe self-contained place to exist, it was de-materialised into an **ecological niche** – a crevice of the ecosystem which provides all the needs of a particular organism.

Figures of speech which have been recently elaborated into scientific models are altogether less dormant and less in need of revival. To speak of an enzyme and its substrate as fitting like a lock and key provokes immediate thought. Suppose we had a key that was not quite the right shape; it might jam up the lock . . . and so we gain a way of understanding the interference caused by substances that are chemically similar to the normal substrate, and we get interested in their molecular shape.

Some figurative origins in scientific words are disguised under Greek derivations. The **hydrophilic** parts of our common detergents have certainly been thought of as 'water-loving', water-seeking, **water-clinging** structures, and we need that idea to understand how a detergent is able to make a 'water-hating' oil drop disperse so readily in a watery world. The Greek-derived word can be activated simply by putting it into other English forms. However, if we are afraid that pupils will 'run away with' the anthropomorphic connotations of the more everyday words, we may keep more closely to the technical one, and in doing so lose some of the mental activation. Too much fear of metaphor is therefore not a help in teaching.

A summary of the figurative word-cycle

Human beings figure things out with the aid of figures of speech. These tease the mind and yield new insights. If we like what we hear we continue to use these words and make them habitual.

Sometimes the new way of speaking can be elaborated into a model to guide prediction and various forms of experimental test, and in science if those tests support the scheme we have developed we stick with it even more strongly, and may come to believe in its reality. In all cases the words which enter into the figurative interaction change their meaning and take on new meanings for the new context of use. Some of them gradually lose their interactiveness and seem after a time to be just ordinary literal words.

How does it matter to science teaching?

If this process is one of the general mechanisms of human intelligence, then pupils will of course be doing some figuring for themselves and it could be important to encourage that and to attend to the words which *they* select as they peruse their squashed onion root or try to make sense of their piece of pumice. However, as I see it, the main consequence for teaching is not to do with their novel figurations, but with how a teacher can help them to understand the ones which are already well established, and see them for what they are.

It would be absurd to expect pupils to work out for themselves all the specialised ways of speaking which generations of thoughtful human beings have built up, so the view of language which I have been outlining leaves no doubt that there is a didactic job to be done by teachers. We do have to show the learners how people formerly thought and spoke and how people think and speak now, and why. This is not so much 'telling' them as helping them to enter imaginatively into the various systems of speech and thought. We can do it by striving *to reactivate the dormant metaphors*. For example, modern children are not of their own initiative going to talk about **harnessing** a waterfall, but they are capable of getting the idea – once they know how culturally important was the change from dependence on horses to other means of getting useful work done. We can help them understand the thoughts behind capturing water in a reservoir and making it 'work for you' with a wheel. We can help them to see that through such

Some ideas connected with the word 'figure'

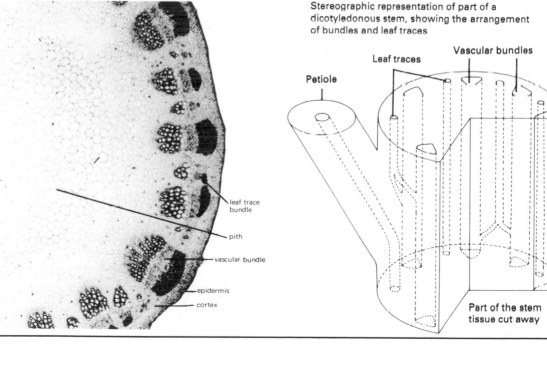

A number (3×10^5)

A digit

To reason something out/to think/to ponder

A sketch

To calculate

Figure-ground perception

An outline

FIGURE

Figure of speech

A human shape

A statue/a form

A diagram in a book

A design

A vague shape seen in fog

A moving pattern in a dance

How can we 'figure out' the meaning of a flat diagram such as a photomicrograph of a cross-section of a plant stem? The authors of the book has helped us part way by linking it to a three dimensional drawing, but we still have to build in our own minds its relationship with a real plant stem. (After C. J. Clegg and Gene Cox in *Anatomy and Activity of Plants* (1978), published by John Murray.)

leaf trace bundle

pith

vascular bundle

epidermis

cortex

Stereographic representation of part of a dicotyledonous stem, showing the arrangement of bundles and leaf traces

Leaf traces

Vascular bundles

Petiole

Part of the stem tissue cut away

efforts **work** started to become a measurable commodity, for which measuring units were needed. That in turn necessitated ways of talking about how fast the work was done as well as how much was achieved, and by this route our modern systems of distinguishing **work** and **power** can gradually be understood.

I hope that I have given enough examples to convince the reader that non-literal language is important in learning and in science. I will end this chapter by wondering how its various forms ever came to be called *'figures* of speech'. For many years **figure** itself was a dormant word for me, one that I used and took for granted, not knowing or caring why or how it came to serve the purposes it does serve. A short enquiry however reveals an unexpected richness. As a noun, the word figure can be used in connection with:

- a line drawing
- the outline of the human body
- a statuette
- a number
- a digit in a number
- an illustration in a book (Fig. 1)
- a silhouette standing out against something else
- a vague shape in the fog or in the flames of a fire
- a transient shape traced out by dancers or skaters

and so on. I doubt if this list is exhaustive. In some of these uses we can glimpse the involvement of an active human mind constructing a meaning. From the silhouette we build a known person. With the figure in the fog we impose the idea of the horseman but it turns out to be nothing more than a few wisps of mist. We use the figure in the book to construct an idea of what it represents. As a verb, figure can also be used for many activities:

- to calculate or work with numbers
- to ponder mentally
- to represent in a diagram
- to solve a puzzle

or (as in this chapter), to seek a way of expressing an idea by using words drawn from some other context.

Do all these usages have something in common? The majority contain the idea of finding or making an outline from which the imagination can construct a meaning. Against that background of custom it appears to me that a **figure of speech** similarly offers a sketchy outline from which an alternative meaning may be constructed. 'Figura' is the Latin equivalent of 'schema' in Greek: a pattern of organised thought, a system of understanding. Figuration is not just passively seeking something which is already there, but is the process of imposing a meaning, or constructing one, or choosing one of several alternative meanings. Alternative metaphors steer one to alternative systems of understanding, and this is why the figurative process is so important in the development of science, and in the development of each new learner's systems of thought. Choosing a different metaphor is in effect choosing an alternative theory.

Notes

1 Figurative language as a general term: At some stage (but not in this book!) it will be appropriate to consider whether or not all the traditional 'figures of speech' can justifiably be lumped together as regards their cognitive function. The case would be that they all work by provoking uncertainty, but I recognise that in this chapter I am mostly referring to a small range of 'figures' – metaphors, similes, parables, and their elaborations as models, analogies and allegories. Most of the literature I quote in this bibliography treats the topic as being 'metaphor' rather than 'figuration'. Nevertheless the larger term seems better as I work towards the implications for science teaching.

2 (a) Interactive views of how metaphors work and what they do:

I. A. Richards (1936) *The Philosophy of Rhetoric*, Oxford University Press
Max Black (1962) *Models and Metaphors*, Cornell University Press
Donald Schon (1963) *Displacement of Concepts*, Tavistock Publications, reissued 1967 as *Invention and the Evolution of Ideas*

It is Schon who most clearly identifies active metaphors as part of a general process of innovation in thought. How can we develop any new ideas except by transferring or transposing old ones onto our current problems? We do it when inventing new technical devices (for example the first railway signals and even the first car direction indicators were based on a raisable arm) but we also do it with words. With the rise of writing 'leaf' was taken over as a reasonable word for the piece of material on which to write and 'quill' for the instrument with which to write, though the quill gradually became less and less feathersome. More recently I notice that 'quill' has been further re-applied and it is now the name for an item of word-processing software.

Black and Schon both contributed to one of the best known collections of essays on the topic: A. Ortony (ed.) (1979) *Metaphor and Thought*, Cambridge University Press.

Recent overviews which bear upon science education include the following, and of these the first is particularly succinct:

Geoffrey N. Cantor, 'Weighing light: the role of metaphor in eighteenth century optical discourse' in A. E. Benjamin, G. N. Cantor and John R. R. Christie (eds) (1987) *The Figural and the Literal*, Manchester University Press.

James J. Bono, 'Science discourse and literature: The role/rule of metaphor in science' in Stuart Peterfreund (ed.) (1990) *Literature and Science*, Northeastern University Press.

C. R. Sutton (1978) *Metaphorically Speaking: The role of metaphor in teaching and learning science*, Leicester University School of Education Occasional Papers.

For a fuller discussion of scientific models in relation to metaphor, see Max Black's book (above) and Mary Hesse (1966) *Models and Analogies in Science*, University of Notre Dame Press, Indiana, and also J. Martin and Rom Harré (1982) 'Metaphor in science' in David S. Miall (ed.) *Metaphor: Problems and Perspectives*. Martin and Harré regard models as non-linguistic.

(b) Root metaphors: In this chapter I have been concerned with the process by which metaphors are generated and appreciated rather than with the nature of the particular metaphors chosen. A large part of the literature on the topic is however concerned to identify and to scrutinise the underlying themes which influence human theorising, the images employed in developing particular scientific, social or political theories, the myths, plots and stories which have influenced people's belief systems and ways of reasoning.

For example, the image of a balance and its associated language of 'weighing up' and comparing the two 'sides' has been used repeatedly. It influences theories in areas as widely different as justice, economics, and chemical reactions. To trace the origins of influential metaphors involves a consideration of the cultural resources available in a particular society, the technologies used, and the social organisation of that society. This emphasis on what the influential metaphors are and where they come from can be found in the second half of Schon's book, in several of the contributions to Ortony's volume, and also in the following:

George Lakoff and Mark Johnson (1981) *Metaphors We Live By*, University of Chicago Press.

Gillian Beer (1983) *Darwin's Plots: Evolutionary Narrative in Darwin, George Eliot and Nineteenth Century Fiction*, Routledge and Kegan Paul.

W. Taylor (1988) 'Metaphors of educational discourse' in W. Taylor, R. K. Elliot, Liam Hudson, David Aspin, Kenneth Charlton and Denis Lawton, *Metaphors of Education*, Heinemann.

G. J. Holton (1973) *Thematic Origins of Scientific Thought*, Harvard University Press.

B. Barnes (1974) *Scientific Knowledge and Sociological Theory*, Routledge and Kegan Paul.

The range of sources available for the figurative transfer of words has consequences for an understanding of the particular models adopted by scientific communities in the past, and probably also for understanding how today's children interpret their world.

(c) Physicists and metaphor: The practice of physics has so often been associated with the feeling of 'firm realities' and 'investigating the world as it really is' that there is a touch of embarrassment in encountering titles such as:

Physics as Metaphor by Richard Jones (Abacus Books, 1983)

Inventing Reality: Physics as language by Bruce Gregory (Wiley, 1988)

Have such books been stimulated in part by the problems of modern particle physics? The quaint growths of language in that field produced such terms as 'quantum chromodynamics' and 'charm' and 'strangeness' as properties of 'quarks'. They must have caused a few raised eyebrows within the research community as well as outside it, and perhaps they hastened the drift to a less realist metaphysic? Could it be that the ultimate knowables are indeed unknowable after all, and the intermediate knowables formed partly through the medium of language? Both books probe more deeply, however, with a longer historical perspective. Gregory for example shows how Newtonian physics can be seen as the successful development of a new way of talking.

3 Parables: The quotation is from C. H. Dodd (1935) *The Parables of the Kingdom*, Nisbett and Co., London. In writing out the quotation I realise how much I have internalised Dodd's vocabulary about the effects of the language – its arresting effect, its vividness, its teasing function.

4 Active and dormant metaphors (rather than 'live' and 'dead' ones): I take these terms most recently from Katherine Hayles (1990) 'Self-reflexive metaphors in Maxwell's Demon and Shannon's Choice' in Stuart Peterfreund (ed.) (1990) *Literature and Science*, Northeastern University Press. Quite apart from their value in suggesting reactivation as a teaching method, the slow collapse of metaphors to a dormant state offers a means of understanding the evolution of scientific language as a continuous and gradual process. In the nineteenth century both geology and biology abandoned sudden-ist theories in favour of gradualist ones, and a similar thing has happened in the later years of this century in relation to the history of ideas. Kuhn's account of scientific revolutions retained sudden-ist features, while Toulmin's 'evolving populations of concepts' made a marked shift towards a gradualist interpretation. See S. Toulmin (1972) *Human Understanding*, Vol. 1, Clarendon Press, Oxford.

A prelude to Chapter 4   INSPIRATION IN SCIENCE

Two examples of the power of non-literal language and its attendant images

1 The power of the image of the 'tree' of living things

As buds give rise . . .

'As buds give rise by growth to fresh buds, and these, if vigorous, branch out and overtop on all sides many a feebler branch, so by generation I believe it to have been with the great Tree of Life, which fills with its dead and broken branches the crust of the earth, and covers the surface with its ever-branching and beautiful ramifications.'

Charles Darwin, 1859, the end of Chapter 4 of The Origin of Species

2 The idea of packaged biological information

It is raining DNA outside . . .

'It is raining DNA outside. On the bank of the Oxford canal at the bottom of my garden is a large willow tree, and it is pumping downy seeds into the air. There is no consistent air movement, and the seeds are drifting outwards in all directions from the tree. Up and down the canal, as far as my binoculars can reach, the water is white with floating cottony flecks, and we can be sure that they have carpeted the ground to much the same radius in other directions too. The cotton wool is mostly made of cellulose, and it dwarfs the tiny capsule that contains the DNA, the genetic information. The DNA content must be a small proportion of the total, so why did I say that it was raining DNA rather than cellulose? The answer is that it is the DNA that matters. The cellulose fluff, although more bulky, is just a parachute, to be discarded. The whole performance, cotton wool, catkins, tree and all, is in aid of one thing and one thing only, the spreading of DNA around the countryside. Not just any DNA, but DNA whose coded characters spell out specific instructions for building willow trees that will shed a new generation of downy seeds. Those fluffy specks are, literally, spreading instructions for making themselves. They are there because their ancestors succeeded in doing the same. It is raining instructions out there; it's raining programs; it's raining tree-growing, fluff-spreading, algorithms. That is not a metaphor, it is the plain truth. It couldn't be any plainer if it were raining floppy discs.'

Richard Dawkins, 1986, the start of Chapter 5 of The Blind Watchmaker

CHAPTER 4

Delightful deceits in words?

The previous chapter introduced the problem of how non-literal language works – a study which is essential to any general reappraisal of the functions of language in science and learning. That study is not yet complete, because I still have to trace in more detail how figurative speech connects with what we see in the mind's eye. At this point however I want to examine the mistrust which scientists feel for all but the most literal uses of language. I start by returning to the quotation about the first Fellows of the Royal Society, already mentioned in Chapter 1. It is worth repeating here, simply to emphasise the power and persistence of an idea which has been with us for three centuries:

> **Their purpose is . . . to make faithful Records of all the works of Nature . . . And to accomplish this they have indeavour'd to separate the knowledge of nature from the colours of Rhetorick, the devices of Fancy, and the delightful deceit of Fables.**

The extract is taken from Thomas Sprat's *History of the Royal Society*[1], in which he went to some length to describe and to justify the Society's aims and methods. Sprat and his contemporaries were emphatic that metaphors were not only unnecessary for the development of 'natural knowledge', they were positively dangerous, and it is a belief which has persisted ever since. It has helped to sustain and enforce a style which strives for unambiguous meaning expressed as economically as possible. Three hundred years of scientific achievement can surely be taken as evidence that it is a useful tradition, at the very least.

How then is it possible to take serious note of the argument of the previous chapter that figurative language plays a central role in human cognition? We have two seemingly contradictory approaches: 'metaphor should be avoided' and 'metaphor is essential' (essential both for the invention of new ideas and for the imaginative understanding of old ones). A resolution of this contradiction seems particularly important for science teaching. If we value scientific precision, dare we accept the ambiguity inherent in the exploration of a metaphor? To approach an answer, let us first consider the case against them as it was developed in the seventeenth century. Avoid metaphors because they

- are just ornamental. They are, as it were, window dressing for what is to be said, and they are unnecessary because anyone who values plain speech can express the same ideas in simpler ways
- are dangerously attractive and liable to inflame the passions
- encourage idle argumentation and disputation with words about grandiose theories which are unchecked against practical experience and experimental test

We could call these the prohibitions against **ornament**, **deceit** and **disputation**, respectively. I believe that the first is definitely invalid and can now be abandoned without loss to science. The others, however, are still valid, and a modern approach to language in science will require that they be kept in mind, for guidance though not for blind obedience. I think that if we separate the points in this way, it will also be possible to devise an approach to teaching and learning in schools which both preserves the search for unambiguous scientific meanings, and makes full use of the ambiguity that words do have in a natural language.

Ornaments of speech?

To take the first point first, the notion of prettying up one's presentation with metaphors dates back to Aristotle's *Poetics*. Because metaphors have an aesthetic appeal, it was assumed that this must be their sole purpose. Notice however that this appeal itself often arises not so much from any added prettiness as from the new insight offered or the novel thought provoked. An unexpected expression is felt to be apt, or insightful, and it is partly that which gives it beauty. Even where the sound quality of a phrase seems to be the dominant aesthetic feature, it is partly the sense of a fresh understanding which makes a statement attractive, as for example in Tennyson's evocation of a cornfield disturbed by light breezes:

. . . and waves of shadow went over the wheat.

More directly within the development of scientific theory, think of the insight provoked by Boyle's phrase about the **spring of the air**. (Robert Boyle, 1667: *New Experiments Physico-Mechanicall Touching the Spring of the Air and its Effects*.) Is there really a simpler 'literal' way in which this idea could have been expressed? Such apparently literal terms as 'compressibility' are available to us only as an outcome of the discussions which Boyle began. The thoughts provoked by his expression ran on into speculative play with ideas about how the springiness could arise, and they motivated innumerable experiments to check those ideas. The several generations of people who used the somewhat more literal term **elastic aeriform vapours** also owe something to Boyle's choice of word. The Founders of the Royal Society nevertheless professed to eschew what they saw as 'ornaments' of speech.

They wanted a simple descriptive language, **rejecting all amplifications, digressions and swellings of style**. Several of them, including Boyle, were nevertheless adept at employing stylistic devices to communicate their thought, and they were highly persuasive as a result, because the style was part of the thought and its communication.

Deceit and idle disputation

'Persuasion' in the 1660s was what it has been ever since – a *bad bad* thought for 'natural philosophers'. They wanted to derive their knowledge by direct inspection of Nature. Metaphor and figurative language generally were seen as techniques of the art of Rhetoric, and Rhetoric was in their bad books because it appeared to be characteristic of generations of philosophers who had made no enquiries directly in the natural world, by handling things, observing them closely, recording what they thought they saw, and devising experiments. The subject called Rhetoric ought really to have many positive associations for teachers, being 'the study of how to express yourself in such a way as to persuade other people'. Instead it had then, and still has today, a pejorative ring because of the potential for persuasion into error or sterile theory.

Perhaps Sprat and others were justifiably exasperated with the **superfluity of talking** which they felt had characterised previous centuries. The mediaeval disputations and logic-chopping, the flowery mystical language of the alchemists, the constant argumentation from the authority of Aristotle; what good had it been? Add to that 'lately' the Wars of the Roses, the Reformation and the Civil War in England with its associated doctrinal disputes. Surely it would be better to talk of actual observations, and of facts not theories? Sprat had a sense of history in which many centuries had been wasted with Philosophy bogged down in verbal disputation, and he also prized knowledge of particular facts rather than 'airy speculations'. He disliked eloquence even though he realised that he needed to use it himself. At one point his indignation breaks out against **these**

A confusion of two sentiments?

The coat of arms of the Royal Society with the motto adopted in 1662.

NULLIUS IN VERBA

Those who first used it, and many since, would have been conscious of its derivation from a longer statement in the Epistles of Horace (65–8 BC). They would see its meaning as

not bound in subservience (allegiance) *to any master* (any authority)

Modern renderings include:

not bound to swear on the word of any master and *Take nobody's word for it.*

However, there is potentially a confusion of two feelings and their attendant meanings:

- one to do with distrust of received opinion which has not been checked against observation or experiment. ('Don't be a slavish follower of what it says in some book; take nobody's word for it; check it yourself!')
- the other a distrust of words generally ('Put not your trust in words!')

This latter is not the original intended meaning, but it is an idea that was expressed quite strongly during the same years, while the Royal Society was getting going, and as its members were working out the essence of their new approach to knowledge.

I suspect that all readers are potentially affected by the negative ring in the N of 'nullius', and are likely to feel it in association with Verba which in other contexts can just mean 'words'. (How N-ish our negative words are: not, never, nothing, no,

null, nil.) One picks up, therefore, an anti-word feeling. To readers unlearned in Latin the motto suggests strongly a distrust of words; it looks and sounds like 'Nothing in words'[3], but if someone had chosen the anti-word idea for an heraldic device they would probably have written **NIHIL IN VERBIS**. In contradiction of any such idea, my own preferred message for learners today would be 'Out of words, many things have come' or even, more strongly:

*Out of words, many **things** have been brought into being*

Having considered the subject with two friends[4], I believe this might be expressed as:

EX VERBIS MULTAE RES GENITAE SUNT

---

specious Tropes or Figures . . . this vicious abundance of Phrase, this trick of Metaphors, this volubility of tongue.

About 25 years after the foundation of the Royal Society, John Locke was writing his *Essay concerning Human Understanding* and he was even less restrained. Rhetoric, he wrote, is **for nothing else but to insinuate wrong ideas, move the passions, and thereby mislead the judgement**. It is **in all discourses that pretend to inform or instruct, wholly to be avoided** and is **a powerful instrument of error and deceit**[2]. His tirade is scarcely less emotive, rhetorical or figurative than a speech by Senator McCarthy about 'Reds under the bed', and like those speeches it is an 'essai' in ways of seeing a problem. Like them it comes to a simplistic conclusion, and once this way of seeing has taken hold it can hardly be shaken off, and the speaker waxes more and more eloquent in elaboration of the theme.

The second of the three criticisms I listed thus seems to be true – even of the critics. New metaphors are indeed powerfully persuasive. They win people's adherence, and even devotion. Marxists see the world through the interpretive language of economic determinacy. Monetarists see it in terms of a neat theory of money supply. Nearer to science a recent example of a compelling figuration is Richard Dawkins' image of the 'selfish gene' and the associated idea of organisms as 'throw-away survival machines' for the perpetuation of those genes. Whether or not it is fully defensible, the power of this image is very great and Dawkins is evidently carried along by it. Another well-known example is the way in which (after Harvey and Descartes) those who accepted the idea of the human body as a machine found it so gripping that previous conceptions of the body were almost unimaginable. Another example from today concerns the way we now use more and more of the language of computers when talking about human reasoning – information stores, parallel processing systems, etc. It becomes hard to avoid the feeling that the brain must be a computer. 'Beware of metaphor' is therefore sound advice. You may get an insight, but who is to say that the insight is valid? You are liable to be drawn into devotion to the particular way of thinking and talking, so that you regard it as the only possible system, the truth. It becomes 'real' for you. Look back at the two examples in the Prelude to this chapter. Darwin wrote about the Tree of Life: 'I believe this simile largely speaks the truth', and Dawkins is so captivated by his new way of seeing that he says: 'That is not a metaphor, it is the plain truth'.

The Natural Philosophers of Charles II's time need not have worried too much about metaphor had their philosophy of science been nearer to that of our own time. They almost had one of the most important remedies for undisciplined metaphor, which is to say, **make sure your way of talking generates testable predictions**, then we can check it by experiment. However, prediction from theory was not yet the most explicit part of their system.

Their view of how theory and experiment were related was often the other way around. Strongly influenced by Francis Bacon, Sprat described the early Fellows as keen to get on with the **observation of Nature in its particulars**, in a variety of fact-gathering expeditions, exercising **a long forbearing of speculation at first, till matters be ripe for it**. That would be . . . **when they have got a sufficient store for such a work** (Sprat, page 107). For all who believed this to be their mode of working, there would be little pressure to articulate their own preliminary theories, and there would seem to be an immediate contrast between themselves as collectors of facts, and others as empty theorisers and word-spinners. In this century the Baconian picture of science as proceeding from particular facts to general laws and hence to greater theories is no longer accepted. More emphasis is given to the testing of predictions from theoretical models. It is therefore easier for us to have a less rejecting attitude to the persuasive powers of metaphor because we now have several ways of screening out the 'worse' from the 'better' metaphors.

Perhaps the dominant feeling in the early scientific communities was a distrust of theory unchecked by observation and experiment. This spilled over into hostility to metaphors, and even to words generally. 'Don't take other people's word for it', 'Don't go by someone's authority, but check it for yourself' slipped towards an associated sentiment 'Words are untrustworthy: put your trust in things'. It seems to me that while the first of these is crucial to the development of science, the second is an unfortunate mistake! (See the panel on previous page: 'A confusion of two sentiments?')

Although it is easier now to recognise the cognitive importance of metaphors, their careful scrutiny and criticism is no less important. Consider some examples from politics and journalism: 'This . . . is undermining our national life . . .', '. . . sapping our lifeblood'. Graphic they may be, emotive and dangerous they are likely to be, but testable they are not. Journalists have recently taken up the graphic and emotive description of a **'hole' in the ozone layer**. This also could be so emotive that it would over-ride rational judgement, but its capacity to mobilise people's feelings might be regarded in this case as valuable rather than pernicious. It does at least have the merit of generating testable predictions.

What about the following expressions which have provided other insights and ways of looking at things? Should they be welcomed or shunned? In what contexts? By what criteria can we judge them: **global village, classroom climate**? What about these from the expanding vocabulary of the computer software writers: **disc doctor, electronic font foundry**? What about this from the world of electronics and radio: **white noise**?

If figurative speech is to be accepted and used more effectively for the exploration of ideas in classrooms there is a need for criticism of any metaphor. That includes asking about its testability, considering alternatives, and making judgements of its aptness as well as of its logic. It involves the sceptical doubting taught in the scientific tradition, but not just instant rejection.

More about scepticism

Peter Medawar, in a characteristically uncomplicated account of science[5] distinguished two important activities within it: **guesswork** (forming new theories) and **checkwork** (experimental testing of consequences, building up evidence for or against).

Science education up to the present day has been dominated by a careful training for the second stage, and hence a sceptical approach to language has predominated. It suits well the professional training of future scientists, for far more of their time will be spent upon that aspect of scientific work. For the education of the general citizen however, the systems for checking knowledge are not really so overwhelmingly important, and experience of them can hardly count as 'education' if the learners never really grasped the ideas in the first place.

It is to enhance the appreciation of ideas that we need a less Spartan attitude to language in science teaching. We do have to teach *ideas* as well as

evidence, and for this we should be more tolerant of metaphors, and of the ambiguity and indefiniteness which words have while you are thinking yourself into a new set of ideas. Caution and scepticism are necessary but not sufficient. For some ways of speaking it really is permissible to let yourself be persuaded by them. In a school context there is also this positive value to the persuasive power of a metaphor which is fully entered into – it does at least engage the learner's feeling as well as his or her mind.

> HEALTH WARNING. Though metaphors can provide you with insights, they may also 'grab your mind' and damage your judgement. Before opening any metaphor, consider how you might test its validity.

Notes

1 Thomas Sprat (1667) *History of the Royal Society of London*, reprinted 1959 by Routledge and Kegan Paul.

2 John Locke (1690) *An Essay concerning Human Understanding*, Dent edition edited by John W. Yolton (1961). The quotations are from Book III (pp. 105–6). Consigning figurative expression as one of the 'imperfections' of language was part of his general plea that words should have constant significations.

3 Interpretations of the sentiment in 'Nullius in Verba': See Allison Coudert (1980) *Alchemy: The philosopher's stone*, Wildwood House, London, p. 216, and Peter Dear (1985) 'Totius in Verba', *Isis*, **76**, 145–61. His title is a play on the motto, picking up the second of the two ways of construing its meaning, in a seeming inversion of it. (P. Dear 1990, personal communication.) Direct statements reading it as NIHIL IN VERBIS are made by Derek Hirst (1986) *Authority and Conflict – England 1603–1658*, p. 360, and Lawrence Goldman (1991) 'Statistics in the science of society in early Victorian Britain', *Social History of Medicine*, **4**, 3, p. 433.

More information about the coat of arms and motto is given by Michael Hunter (1989) in *Establishing the New Science*, Boydell Press. He shows the notes on alternative designs sketched by John Evelyn when plans for a coat of arms were made. One of the possibilities considered was 'Omnia Probate' – 'Try all things' or 'Check all things' (with the implication of 'holding fast to that which is good', which survives your checking). The words allude to St. Paul's First Epistle to the Thessalonians, Chapter 5 verses 19–20 and it is interesting to note the two alternative translations of this which are now offered in the *New English Bible*: 'Do not stifle inspiration, and do not despise prophetic utterances, but bring them all to the test and then keep what is good in them . . .' or else 'Put everything to the test; keep hold of what is good . . .'

Dorothy Stimpson in her history of the Royal Society reports a quip made on St. Andrew's Day 1663 when the Society was meeting for elections. Responding to a query about whether in England St. George's Day would not be more appropriate for such an important event, one of the Fellows is reported as saying: *I had rather have had it been on St. Thomas's Day, for he would not beleeve till he had seen and putt his fingers into the holes, according to the motto Nullius in Verba*. See D. Stimpson (1949) *Scientists and Amateurs*, Sigma Books, p. 64.

4 I am grateful to Duncan and Jean Cloud for discussion not only of the original Latin allusion, but of how one might express in Latin the idea that words are often the starting-point for generating things.

5 'Guesswork and checkwork, proposal and disposal. . .': This phrasing was part of Peter Medawar's extemporisation on Karl Popper's 'Conjectures and Refutations'. See P. Medawar (1967) *The Art of the Soluble*, Methuen.

CHAPTER 5

Words, seeing, and seeing as . . .

Why don't we all see the same things when we look at something? And why don't the pupils see what we want them to see? I thought this lesson was about metals reacting with acid, so why has Robert spent so long on drawing the stands which held the apparatus, and Jackie has even lavished loving care on a sketch of the maker's trade mark from the side of the flask? I saw the lesson as about a certain reaction – no, a certain *class* of reactions, and therefore about a chemical principle, but it seems that they saw it as about stands and flasks and jars, tubes and bubbles and pops. Was it my fault for not drawing their attention properly to the central points, to the *contents* of the flask, and the pattern I had in mind? Next time I will tell them to draw just a close-up of a piece of zinc or iron, with the acid around it. Will that enable them to 'see' the metal displacing the hydrogen? Seeing bubbles is not the same as 'seeing' that substance 'displaced' from the acid.[1]

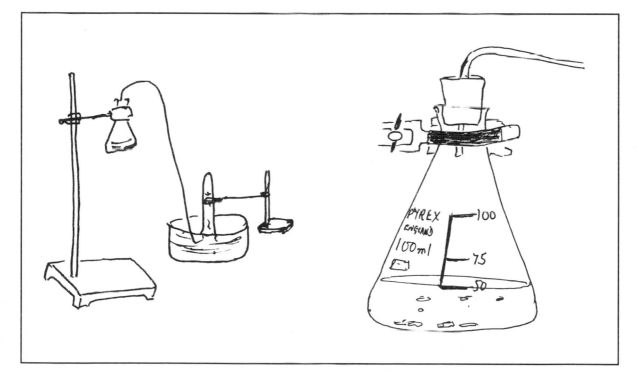

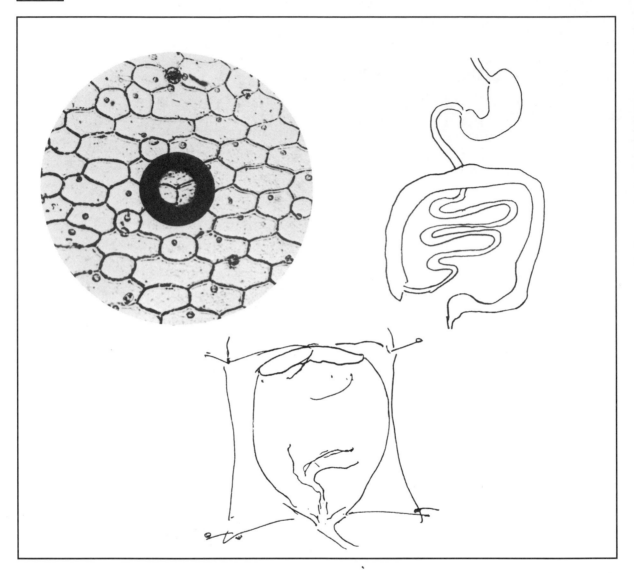

Certainly it is my responsibility to guide their eyes, but can I really control what they see as significant, and what they understand it to mean? I remember their response to the dissected abdomen of a rat (when the Ughs were over), and how I only got 'decent' diagrams by allowing them to copy from the book rather than from the dissection. We did get slightly better sketches when I made the theme of the lesson 'searching for the path which the food takes'. Words are important in guiding perception, and then at least they did all show continuity from stomach to rectum.

The microscope has been another area of difficulty – I think of their drawings of the bubbles on the slide, which I thought I had told them to ignore. How did I ever expect them to 'see' the jiggety-jiggety Brownian motion of smoke particles as an effect of assumed molecular bombardment rather than as glow-worms animated with their own motion? I know now though! Preparing their minds to 'see' the particles suffering this random bombardment takes time and much work on their imagination beforehand.

One problem is that the dominant traditions of

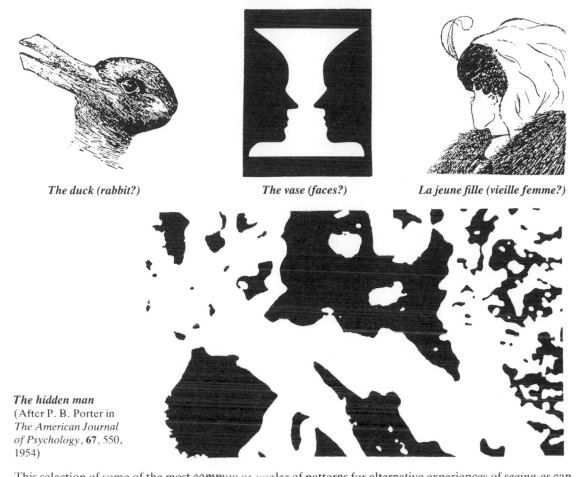

The duck (rabbit?)   *The vase (faces?)*   *La jeune fille (vieille femme?)*

The hidden man
(After P. B. Porter in
*The American Journal
of Psychology*, **67**, 550,
1954)

This selection of some of the most common examples of patterns for alternative experiences of *seeing-as* can hardly do justice to the topic. They are included as a reminder for those already familiar with the phenomenon, but readers are recommended to look closely at commentaries by Gregory and by Hanson on the Ames room, on impossible shapes, on the drawings of M. C. Escher, and other examples.[3,5]

science teaching are so strong: 'Draw what you see . . . Just describe what you see . . . Say what happened . . . Write down your observations.' They continue to influence day-to-day life in classrooms[2] even though a more sophisticated understanding of seeing has been available for decades. It is over 30 years now since a Yale University philosopher, N. R. Hanson, wrote (drawing on the American vocabulary of those days):[3]

There is more to seeing than meets the eyeball.

Hanson presented his argument with conviction and humour, tight logic, and a wealth of supporting evidence, but philosophers influence practice only slowly. The 'findings' of psychology work faster on the public imagination however, and it is the concept of the 'Gestalt' which has had the greatest effect in bringing about a re-appraisal of what 'seeing' involves. Ducks and rabbits; faces and vases; old women and young ones; what are we doing when we 'see' something which others do not see, or when we switch from one way of seeing to another? Gestalt psychology made us think about this. For one writer[4] it led straight to a questioning of teaching methods, but its implications for science teaching have been worked out by a longer route which involves the philosophy of science. Psychology of perception, philosophy of science, and the sociology and history of science came together. Hanson brought the study of perception to bear upon the philosophy of science, and I have borrowed and extended one of his titles to make the title of this chapter. He showed very clearly that 'seeing as' involves prior experience as well as what is actually on the retina.

The basic idea of perception of 'Gestalts' originated in Germany in the 1920s, but some of the most compelling demonstrations of how important the effect is were developed in the USA in the 1950s by Adelbert Ames. With devices such as the one in which a viewer looks at a distorted room he suggested very effectively that perception is not a passive process at all but a highly active one in which the brain of the person who is seeing contributes far more than had been commonly thought. In Britain the phenomenon was brought to the attention of a much wider public in the 1960s and 1970s in two books by Richard Gregory – *Eye and Brain* and *The Intelligent Eye*.[5]

To say that knowledge is not gained simply by passive attention to the evidence of one's senses was not entirely novel. It had been suggested in the last century, but the idea had never gained wide acceptance (at least in science teaching) before these studies of 'active seeing'. It was somehow overwhelmed by a dominant view that facts are facts to be noted by straightforward observation. Using your senses as 'the inlets of knowledge' (John Locke's expression) seemed to be a self-evident part of being scientific. However, once the experiences of active seeing were widely available, an alternative view could not be ignored. The act of seeing was understood in a new way, with the seer contributing something very important in order to make sense of 'what is there'.

In the writings of Hanson and others all this helped to consolidate the changes which had long been going on in how science is described, with much less emphasis on accumulation of experience and more on the interplay of theory and specu-

lation with that experience. Conscious conjectures to be tested were more readily recognised as a key element. That is what is now called the hypothetico-deductive view of science. Peter Medawar, in *The Art of the Soluble*, surveys earlier enunciations of it by William Whewell (1794–1866) and W. S. Jevons (1835–82), well before the better known analysis by Karl Popper (1902–). With the benefit of what we now know about perception, Whewell's statement seems particularly useful today:

> **Facts cannot be observed as Facts except in virtue of the Conceptions which the observer himself supplies**

Ways of seeing: the seer's contribution

So what exactly does the observer, the seer, contribute? A disturbing feature of the Gestalt effect was that making sense of what had previously been called 'illusions' (mock games played by your mind, pretences, deceits) could suddenly be understood as the same kind of activity as making sense of what we believe is really there. Illusion became just a special case of vision in general. In both cases what we see depends on our existing state of mind.

There seem to be at least two different kinds of experience which can affect the seer and enable him or her to go 'beyond the information given':

(i) Influences from previous experience, of which one is hardly aware and over which one has little control,

(ii) Influences from theories, belief systems, and *ways of talking*. These are more open to modification, at least in principle.

As an example of the first (unconscious) influence, consider the two walls in the adjacent panel. To see the mortar as protruding or recessed could result from having been long accustomed to certain shadow patterns. Usually without realising it we apply that previous experience to make sense of the pictures. Try not doing so. Try making either picture look as flat as it actually is on the paper. So powerful has the habit become that it is almost impossible to escape some depth effect.

Two walls? Or two ways of seeing one wall?

What do we 'see' in the distribution of the mortar between the bricks? To see it as oozing out, or eroded away, involves past experience of such sights. Habitual ways of seeing may involve an assumption (hardly conscious) that when dark areas appear below a feature they indicate shadows of something which protrudes. Gregory wrote of 'the intelligent eye'; here we have 'an accustomed eye'. Turn the page upside down to get an alternative impression. (Photograph: Ray Hemmings and M. Bonsor.)

As an example of the second kind of influence, consider the earlier panel on p. 37, and notice how a word – **faces** or **vase**, can act as an organiser or re-organiser in how you see one of the patterns. Or consider how we may gaze at the bark of a tree trunk, and a few words from a trained observer (with or without the word 'camouflage') can suddenly reveal to others the hitherto unsuspected moths, now blending in, now leaping out for the educated eye.

This latter situation is of most interest for science and for education because the 'theories' or 'frameworks of understanding' involved are capable of change. The ability of geologists to 'see' the signs of glaciation in mountain valleys changed markedly during the nineteenth century. A school learner today can experience a similar development in seeing ability with comparatively little help. Indeed, after a few days of study of such valleys the single word **glaciation** can come to sum up a whole system of thought. The interplay of a word with the system of imagery it calls up seems to be very important both in 'discovery' and in 'learning', yet it has not been adequately explored in relation to our teaching methods.

Ways of seeing: their resistance to change

Although alteration is possible, there is also a tendency not to alter. A way of seeing and its associated way of talking can be very self-preserving. Especially when we consider 'mind's eye' seeing rather than that which involves the eyes directly,[1] existing theories maintain themselves and direct what we attend to, and also what we *do not* attend to. If you lived in the days before Queen Elizabeth and William Harvey and you thought of the blood as 'liquid food' renewed from the stomach, you might easily see it as flowing continuously from the gut to feed parts of the body. You would then have no need of any enquiry into its 'circulation around' the body, no need to wonder about the structures in the veins which we now see to be one-way valves, no need to speculate about unseen connections from arteries to veins. Jumping to the present day, if you are a child who believes that electricity gets weaker along a wire, then you may continue to see it weakening as it gets further from the battery and hardly notice what a teacher is saying about the 'electric current' being the same all round the circuit.

Persuasion into new views

Nevertheless, ways of seeing do change and it is possible to be persuaded into a new way of seeing, using a combination of words and evidence, as when William Harvey (1578–1657) wondered about the blood having **motion, as it were in a circle**. This phrasing, together with his calculations of how much blood could leave a chamber of the heart in half an hour, was compelling. It led to seeing the structures in the veins as one-way valves, and the musculature of the heart as highly significant. Later this whole system of seeing steered Malpighi's eyes towards the mini-pipes in a tadpole's tail which demonstrated the completeness of the circuit. Harvey himself groped towards an understanding of that connection with a usefully vague image, describing the blood as going into the tissues as into **a sponge**, and then later draining from them into veins as water is collected by drainage pipes from **a swamp**.

Words steer perception both positively and negatively, and also they influence what people do or do not do as well as what they see or miss seeing. The **inert gases** were hardly investigated for chemical re-activity at all because the name, and the whole structure of thought in which it was embedded suggested it would not be worth doing so. When however there was a shift in understanding partly on theoretical grounds, and some of them were found to be reactive at least towards fluorine it stimulated a flurry of enquiries. They were then renamed the **noble gases**, incidentally consolidating the chemical meaning of 'noble' as 'not very reactive', like the noble metals platinum and gold.

Sadi Carnot, writing in 1824 about the theoretical principles of steam engines and heat engines generally, was guided by his image of **the fall of the heat** from a higher 'level' (higher temperature) to a lower one, and what he was able to do therefore was to apply reasoning to it about the limits to the useful work it would do, just as he could to the fall of water in a waterfall of a certain height.

Selecting a new metaphor is one of the main tools of innovation in thought. It makes familiar things less taken for granted, and draws our attention to different aspects of the topic. Once Harvey saw the heart **as a pump** or Darwin saw the 'tree of life' **as a branching pattern through the generations**, there were a host of new questions which could be investigated. Hence we find this kind of redescription marks many of the crucial moments of change in scientific thought, and it leads on to many new experimental enquiries. It is by entering imaginatively into the new way of seeing that we become able to suggest ways of checking it, or to appreciate those suggested by other people.

One example which used to be well known as a considerable cultural and scientific achievement was the realisation by Torricelli and others that we live **at the bottom of an ocean of air**[6]. At the time, the implications of this way of seeing multiplied rapidly. They motivated expeditions up and down mountains with columns of mercury, calculations of how far up the 'ocean' might extend, and many other inquiries. For an indication of what might be involved in getting youngsters to see the atmosphere in this way, and to feel it as **the atmosphere**, not just 'the air', consider this passage written in 1878. It could be worth holding back the barometers and the worksheets for a while, until pupils have had a chance to respond to this verbal/visual theorising (see adjacent panel).

Learning to see

Learning science involves learning to see in new ways:

- Seeing the salt as **dissolving** (and not just disappearing), seeing that it could be recovered from the interstices of the liquid
- Seeing the **circuit** amongst the tangle of wires, seeing the plastic as an insulator, seeing the need for continuity in a circuit and therefore knowing where to check for breaks

Arabella Buckley (1878) takes time and space to gain an imaginative understanding of 'the ocean of air'

THE AERIAL OCEAN IN WHICH WE LIVE

Did you ever sit on the bank of a river in some quiet spot where the water was deep and clear, and watch the fishes swimming lazily along? When I was a child this was one of my favourite occupations in the summer time on the banks of the Thames, and there was one question which often puzzled me greatly, as I watched the minnows and gudgeon gliding along through the water. Why should fishes live in something and be often buffeted about by waves and current, while I and others lived on the top of the earth and not in anything? I do not remember ever asking anyone about this; and if I had, in those days people did not pay much attention to children's questions, and probably nobody would have told me, what I now tell you, that we do live in something quite as real and often quite as rough and stormy as the water in which the fishes swim. The something in which we live is air, and the reason that we do not perceive it, is that we are in it, and that it is a gas, and invisible to us; while we are above the water in which the fishes live, and it is a liquid which our eyes can perceive.

But let us suppose for a moment that a being, whose eyes were so made that he could see gases as we see liquids, was looking down from a distance upon our earth. He would see an ocean of air, or aerial ocean, all round the globe, with birds floating about in it, and people walking along the bottom, just as we see fish gliding along the bottom of a river.

- Seeing the **food** of an animal as a **fuel**, and its **respiration** as a form of **combustion**
- Seeing a flame as a **reaction zone** – imagining the agitated fuel and oxygen molecules churning together, colliding, breaking, reassembling as carbon dioxide and water
- 'Seeing' the **ions migrating** in the electrolysis vessel, and therefore knowing what to look for at each electrode

Just a valley?
(Photograph: Patrick Bailey)

Just a test tube?
(From a colour photograph by M. Bonsor)

Just a moth?
(Photograph courtesy of H. B. D. Kettlewell and W. H. Dowdeswell)

What do we need behind our eyes to 'see' the signs of glaciation in the valley, or the moth-ness of *both* moths, or the alleged whiteness of a 'precipitate' in the test tube? 'What else do we need in order to 'see' the long-melted glaciers that swamped the valley, to discern a relationship between the moths, or to recognise an insoluble substance 'thrown down' as the result of a chemical reaction?

(To appreciate the problem of making sense of the contents of the test tube, take a blue solution of copper chloride, and add drops of silver nitrate solution to it. Convince yourself that you have a *white* solid floating in a *blue* solution. How do you do so, and how do you recognise where that solid came from?)

Each of these ways of seeing extends the power of what Hanson called the 'spectacles behind the eyes' of the learner. In other words, if the teacher succeeds in communicating the new 'insights', they can gradually be used as 'outlooks', an extra means by which the learner can interpret further experience.[7] Each of them is more sophisticated than the ways of seeing which a child learns in the pram, enabling her to 'see' brick walls and such like. They will not spring automatically from a small amount of practical experience at the bench, but require a careful exploration of the ways of talking which form our science.

Notes

1 Seeing and comprehending: It might be objected that I slip too easily between a literal use of 'see' (something involving the eyes) and what would formerly have been called a metaphorical use ('seeing in the mind's eye' or 'comprehending', as in the expression 'Oh I see what you mean'). However, it seems to me that all the studies of the 'eye-and-brain-together' make it much more difficult to maintain a distinction between eye activities and brain activities. Richard Gregory suggests that in human evolution thinking has emerged from seeing (p. 143 of *The Intelligent Eye* – the full reference is given in Note 5 below). 'I see' or 'I gain an insight' is certainly a very special metaphor if it is a metaphor at all!

In the previous chapters on figurative speech I was conscious of the difficulty of keeping words about understanding separate from those associated with visual imagery, and I still find it hard to draw any firm line between 'comprehension' and 'insight':

comprehension → cognitive appreciation → new ways of seeing (– new 'understanding') → 'insight'

Similarly 'metaphor' – so apparently linguistic – is often replaced easily by 'image', so apparently visual:

metaphor ⟶ image

Perhaps we are just trapped in a completely circular way of talking? Even the word 'apparently' in the last sentence is a visual word. Will there be any resolution of this problem when neurophysiologists can tell us more about how different areas of the cerebral cortex affect each other? See Colin Blakemore (1988) *The Mind Machine*, BBC Books, pp. 145–6.

2 Traditions of school writing: data before theory. See C. R. Sutton (1989) 'Writing and reading in science: the hidden messages' in Robin Millar's *Doing Science: Images of Science in Science Education*, Falmer Press.

3 'More to seeing than meets the eyeball': This phrase was used by N. R. Hanson in his 1958 book *Patterns of Discovery*, Cambridge University Press. A further development of the same themes is found in N. R Hanson (1969) *Perception and Discovery*, Freeman Cooper & Co., San Francisco. This includes chapters on 'Seeing as' and 'Seeing that', and on the changes that hypotheses make in our apprehension of 'facts'.

4 Teaching methods affected by how we understand seeing: see M. L. J. Abercrombie (1960) *The Anatomy of Judgment*, Hutchinson. Republished in 1969 by Penguin Books.

5 Studies of 'active seeing' brought to a wider audience: Adelbert Ames' distorted rooms and other demonstrations are discussed by Hanson and by Abercrombie in the above books, but probably the most accessible sources are now Richard Gregory's books *The Intelligent Eye* (1970) and *Eye and Brain* (1966) both published by Weidenfeld and Nicolson.

6 The 'ocean of air': For a recent account see Joan Solomon (1989) *The Big Squeeze*, Association for Science Education, Hatfield. For Arabella Buckley's evocative re-creation of the idea see *The Fairyland of Science* (1878), Edward Stanford, London.

7 'Insights' becoming 'outlooks': I associate this phrase with Arthur Koestler (1949) as the title of the book which he re-wrote later and published as *The Act of Creation* (1964). His concept of three kinds of creativity (scientific, artistic, comic), which all involve 'bi-sociation' of ideas from 'planes of meaning' that were previously separate has much to offer as another way of imagining key aspects of metaphorical redescription. With the phrase 'insight and outlook' he also captured in more ordinary language the idea of 'constructing and construing' which is central to George Kelly's 'Personal Construct Theory'. (See discussion later in this book, Chapter 12.)

A NOTE TO THE READER

The question discussed in Chapter 5 – how seeing connects with the theories one holds and the ways of talking one chooses – could take us into current philosophical problems about the basis of firm knowledge, i.e. what a **theory** is, what characterises a good **scientific theory**, what we mean by **discovery**, what a **fact** is, and so on. If you want to consider those aspects more fully, you may like to go to Chapters 11 and 12 now, and return later to this point.

The changes which have occurred in the meanings of those terms are important to the general theme of this book, but I hope the immediately following Chapters (6–10) will nevertheless make sense on their own if you prefer to take a more direct line towards policies for the classroom. That is what I want to attempt now. Drawing on what I have already said about the kinds of mental agitation which words are capable of producing, how can we understand better what is going on in science classrooms?

CHAPTER 6

Ways of seeing and ways of talking

My view of how people can learn science is based on the linkage between a **new way of seeing** any topic and a **new way of talking** about it. This new way of talking is more than a few extra words; it consists of an extended network of meaningful statements which make sense to those who take on the new way of seeing, and in this short chapter I want to emphasise those networks and connections. For example, once we see a wire as a **conductor**, we are on the way to imagining the transport of something along it, and to composing sentences about flow, easy flow, more difficult flow, tendency to flow, and so on. The word **conductor** depends for its meaning on linked words such as 'flow', and when a cluster of such words is developed to form a way of talking about electricity, the meaning of that key word is further refined by its relationship with the idea of a measured flow, i.e. a **current**, and then with other terms such as **resistance**.

For another example, if we start to see an animal's **food** as a kind of **fuel**, and its **respiration** as a sort of slow **combustion**, then a discussion can be elaborated from our existing connections to 'fuel' and 'combustion'. Innumerable new propositions might be made. We could talk about the functions of inhaling air, about how respiration might be supported inside the body, or about what we would expect to find in the exhaled gases. We could also speak about the energy changes occurring as organised 'food + air' changes into less organised 'products of respiration'.

Single words therefore should not be treated in isolation. They take their meaning from the connections which they have and the kinds of statement into which they may be built. The whole network of connections and assembly of sensible statements can often be understood as being organised by a certain picture or image of what is going on. What we see in the 'mind's eye' appears to steer and shape the manner in which we speak. Consider for example James Hutton's image of 'lofty mountains going into ruin', which is set out in the panel overleaf.

I have argued in previous chapters that an image in the mind's eye can be triggered by a particular choice of words, if the hearer already has some appropriate connections to those words. The image can then guide the selection of further words, and so newly-initiated learners who get the image are able to generate further statements about the topic for themselves. Teacher and learner will end up with the same 'way of talking' if it is based on a coherent image that picks out similar connections for each of them. To improve the learning, we probably need ways of mapping not only the prior connections that words excite, but also the 'mind's eye pictures' that they elicit, and the new connections which are brought to prominence as a result. Approaches to doing so will be explored in Chapter 8; meanwhile it is sufficient to note the grouping of scientific words into coherent networks.

Sometimes a grouping is less obviously based on a visual image, but springs partly from our intuitive grasp of grammar.[1] The noun **magnet** implies not only the adjective **magnetic** but also the verb **to magnetise**. Perhaps however it only does so once

A family of words which have become linked together within a 'way of talking' that is guided by a 'way of seeing'

ERODE EROSION WEATHERING DEPOSIT DEPOSITION SEDIMENT SEDIMENTATION
SEDIMENTARY ROCK   LAYERS OR STRATA

In this case the guiding image is of continuous, uniform, geological processes which are capable of removing rocks from mountains, and which might perhaps account for the formation of new rocks too. It is the start of an image of a 'rock cycle' for certain kinds of rock. Using that picture in the mind's eye, a range of statements may be constructed, e.g.

1 'Rocks in high positions, exposed to weather, are gradually eroded by physical and chemical processes, and the fragments carried away by glaciers and rivers, forming sediments in estuaries and on the sea-floor nearby' *or*
2 'Compacted sediments may gradually form new rock strata'.

The individual words develop specific meanings from their interaction with the others. This way of talking seems to have begun with James Hutton in the latter part of the eighteenth century. He 'saw' the slow processes of 'lofty mountains going into ruin', and began to talk accordingly. Teachers who introduce newcomers to these thoughts nowadays may try to communicate the image in order to give full meaning to the vocabulary.

we allow ourselves to think of making a new magnet, and the extension would not have occurred when the only magnets known were lodestones. Similarly the adjective **immune** might stand alone as a description of a state of exemption from disease, but if we take on the idea that human beings can influence that state, then we can make a verb **to immunise** and a further noun **immunisation**.[2]

More could perhaps be made of these different parts of speech within a science course. Science textbooks traditionally have been rich in abstract nouns (synthesis, heredity, vibration, propagation, decomposition, etc.) rather than in the active verb forms ('we synthesise', 'she inherits', 'it vibrates', 'they propagate', and so on). When Michael Faraday set out his new way of talking about the effects of electricity on chemical substances, he explicitly put down a noun for the material to be decomposed (**electrolyte**) and a verb (**electrolyse**/electrolyze – he spelled it with a 'z'). The abstract name for the overall process (**electrolysis**) followed later as a replacement for the rather clumsy **electrolization**. A whole family of

words was gradually drawn into existence, partly through grammatical and semantic appropriateness, and partly through the powerful imagery which Faraday had of something happening within the body of the decomposing substance and at the surfaces where the electric current was presumed to enter and leave the liquid. Eventually, as already mentioned at the end of Chapter 2, this led him – in consultation with other people – to the invention of the further words **electrode, anode, cathode, ion, anion** and **cation**, thus formulating a way of talking which with a little modification has become the standard parlance today.[3]

A new network changes the meaning of individual words

The interdependence of words for their meaning is a general feature of language, but it has a special relevance in science when the older meanings of pre-existing words are distorted as the words are forced into new uses. An older meaning is often left behind and a new specialised scientific meaning develops for each of several words in the network. For example, the chemical meaning of **a salt** is dependent on the related meaning of **an acid** and **a base**, and Newton's meaning of **force** is dependent on the related meanings of **momentum** and **change of momentum**.

We can see what happens by considering the first of these examples in more detail. **Salt** has long been used for the single substance we now call sodium chloride, and of course in everyday life it still has that meaning. For many centuries however it was not precisely confined to that one substance but also applied to other water-soluble materials, and sometimes to substances with a particular kind of taste.[4] By the seventeenth century it was being applied to many such substances which were artificially prepared rather than naturally occurring, and these were derived from acids. The process of countering the acidity was also seen to be one of the commonest of chemical processes. The word **acid** developed in meaning too, and became associated with non-metallic simple substances, and specifically with what we now call the oxides of non-metallic elements. Their acidity could be **neutralised** by using substances derived from metals (what we now call metal oxides), and chemical books referred to such things as **magnesia – the base of Epsom salt**. While other contemporary terms for groups of chemical substances (e.g. the **earths** or the **calces**) have more or less died out, **base** and **acid** survived as useful generic terms and were made more precise in their application. **Salt** became a generic term for the product of their interaction. The whole system involves the words acid, base, neutralise and neutral, as well as **salt** itself. The new specialised meanings can properly be understood only in the context of statements like: **When an acid is neutralised by a base one of the products is a salt**.

Another instructive pairing in chemistry is the relationship of **balanced** and **equation** as applied to the summary of a chemical process. The guiding image that produced these words was probably from accountancy (balance sheets). You check up that all the inputs are accounted for in the outputs. Both words now have an exact meaning in the context of chemical shorthand which is related to but not the same as their use in everyday life.

In all sections of science we can find developments of specialised meaning in one word by having it placed in a particular relationship with others. The biologist's meaning of a **fruit** (seed container with its seeds) differs from a chef's meaning of **fruit**, because it connects, in ways emphasised by the biologist, with **seed** and flower and **dispersal mechanism**.

Another kind of interdependence of words, common in science but not peculiar to it, is the situation in which pairs of words help to define each other, for example **gametes** and **zygote**. Another is in the generation of general forms from which someone who understands the new way of talking can make additional words of their own. For example, once you accept the system of describing an animal as a **herbivore** or a **carnivore** it is quite feasible to place a borderline case as an omnivore rejoicing in onmiverous life. Facetious pupils might even be ready to think of themselves as 'hamburgivores'.

Teaching the images and the networks of words

The consequences of these considerations for teaching include at least the following:

- It would be sensible to encourage awareness of how words group themselves into families – families connected by a particular image, and also grammatically linked families – noun, verb and adjectival forms.
- A teacher might do better to work on the mind's eye of the pupil, rather than just on the form of what is said. Practical experience and what the teacher says could both be chosen specifically to enrich the visualisation.
- Freedom for pupils to express their own statements in response to their image of what is going on could be particularly important.

My overall conclusion at this stage is that we can think of science teaching as a process of **inducting someone into new ways of seeing and new ways of talking**. The means available are partly experiential and partly linguistic, and both work by developing what the learner 'sees' in his or her mind's eye. Children need tangible experience (for example feeling two magnets pushing each other apart), but it is in grappling with the words about 'repulsion' and 'force diminishing with distance' that they start to build up a fuller image of 'magnetic field', and eventually are able to talk in a similar way themselves.

Notes

1 'Intuitive grammar' or 'images'? What are the mental tools which organise our speech and make it possible to generate new meaningful statements? Scholars of linguistics have been preoccupied for several decades over the question of what 'deep structure' in language might enable people to turn around a statement such as 'Sediments harden and form rocks' and come out with a meaningful transformation like '(Some) rocks are formed from hardened sediments'. A key feature of language is the power which human beings have to make such transformations and to generate new sentences of their own. Many of those new sentences will not have existed before, and yet they are understood as sensible; nonsensical statements seem to have been screened out. Hence it is argued that there must be some 'deep' internal system controlling the generation of what people say. A brief account of these ideas, from the work of Noam Chomsky onwards, is given by David Crystal in the *Cambridge Encyclopaedia of Language* (Cambridge University Press, 1987), p. 409.

The possibilities of transformation, as well as the 'simple' surface grammar of a sentence, must influence how a scientist chooses to express an idea, and how a pupil does so. Because such influence is inexplicit, I have tried to capture it in the expression 'intuitive grammar'. It appears to me, however, that semantic relationships have a very strong controlling influence on what will be said by any human being who 'gets an idea'. That is why I selected a 'mental image', or 'way of seeing' as the internal something which is perhaps monitoring what we feel we can say. I see the mental relationship between 'flow' and 'current' as more significant than that between flow, flowing and flowed, although any complete theory of meaning should include both types of connection.

Further contributions to the understanding of the relationship between a way of talking and a way of seeing might eventually come from neurophysiology, but for the time being it seems to me that an everyday practical system for guiding learners can be constructed around 'what you see in your mind's eye' and 'a family of words and expressions that go with it'.

2 From 'immune' and 'immunity' to 'immunise' and 'immunisation': According to the *Oxford English Dictionary*, the first two of these words have a long history of use in the context of exemption from public service or tax obligations, and of being privileged in that sense. The other two emerged as the germ theory of disease developed towards the end of the nineteenth century, consolidating a larger network of words linked in meaning in the new context of someone 'privileged' or 'exempt' from a disease, and the process of inducing that state.

3 Electrolyte, electrolyse, electrode, anode, cathode, anion, cation, ions: Michael Faraday set out his new system under the title 'On electrochemical decomposition' in the *Philosophical Transactions of the Royal Society* for 1834. The story of the reasoning behind the new words, and of Faraday's discussions with Dr Nicholl and correspondence with William Whewell is told by J. R. Partington in *A History of Chemistry*, Macmillan (1964) Vol. 4, pp. 116–18. The letters exchanged with Whewell are available in L. Pearce Williams' collection (1971) *The Selected Correspondence of Michael Faraday*, Cambridge University Press. The terms considered and rejected are themselves of considerable interest; they included zetode, eisode and exode, Voltode and Galvanode, and electrostechions, as well as Faraday's earlier 'electrobeids'. There have been some developments in meaning since Faraday's time – notably in the term 'ions'; anion and cation are now seen as referring more definitely to charged atoms or groups of atoms migrating through the liquid. The last part of Faraday's summarising sentence in the 1834 paper is not quite what would be said today: 'Thus the chloride of lead is an *electrolyte*, and when *electrolyzed* evolves the two *ions* chlorine and lead, the former being an *anion* and the latter a *cation*'.

4 Salt and acid: A partial account of the development of the specialist meanings of these words is given in M. P. Crosland (1962) *Historical Studies in the Language of Chemistry*, Heinemann, pp. 108–10.

CHAPTER 7

Interpretations and labels

What is language for in science and in teaching? Common sense answers often centre around the notion of 'communicating ideas', with an implication that how that happens will be obvious. I have been saying, on the other hand, that in science it is for '*creating* and communicating ideas', while in teaching it is for '*re-creating* ideas' – a process that is more than 'informing' the learners, and better thought of as inducting them into a certain way of talking about the topic in hand, guided by a particular way of seeing it.

None of these accounts does justice to the social and emotional functions of language, which actually take precedence in the classroom (see pages 79, 102 and 109), but they do start to reveal a contrast in beliefs about how language works in relation to knowledge, information and understanding. In this chapter I want to explore two such views, which seem to arise from two different kinds of use. These two uses are both necessary and inevitable, but I shall argue that one of the associated belief-systems is mistaken, and a hindrance to learning.

Two ways of using language

How can I best characterise the two uses which I have in mind? One is exploratory, the other declarative, one is tentative while the other is definite, and one never takes meaning as obvious, while the other has to do so. To put it another way, sometimes a speaker or writer is aware that there is room for doubt about how an idea shall be expressed, and therefore makes a careful choice of words in order to capture the idea as closely as possible. On other occasions, words seem immediately available and there is scarcely any calculation or choice of what to say. I shall call the first an **interpretive** way of using language – finding the words and seeing them as part of the understanding, and the second a **labelling** way – using them in a relatively automatic manner. Interpretive use of language is consciously a means of helping yourself and other people to see a topic in new ways. Labelling language implies there is only one possible way to see it.

Interpreting and labelling: more examples from science

I have already given examples of interpretive use – for example, Lavoisier's discussion of how to express the idea of 'matter of heat' (see page 13). Here is another, from Robert Hooke's account (1665) of what he saw when looking at thin slices of cork under his microscope. We find him trying out various words to convey the compartmentalisation of the material into millions of little cavities:

> . . . these pores, or cells, were not very deep, but consisted of a great many little Boxes, separated out of one continued long pore, by certain Diaphragms . . . in a Cubick Inch about twelve hundred Millions . . . a thing almost incredible, did not our Microscope assure us of it.

He also tried 'Boxes or Bladders' to convey the porosity of the material, and an image of the units he saw it was composed of, but **cell** was the word which survived best. Hooke took it from earlier uses where it referred to the compartments in a honeycomb, or the monks' rooms in a monastery, and very quickly it came to be the automatic choice when talking about plant tissues or indeed any other biological material under the microscope. In those contexts it became just a label for one of these biological entities. A new meaning for the word 'cell' had emerged, specific to this biological context, and ever since that time people have been able to say things like: **Most plant cells have rather thick cell walls**, or **Look at the cells in this squashed root tip**, with little anxiety over whether their meaning will be understood. The value of this word as an organiser of what we attend to when we now look down a microscope is immense. It shapes how we think as well as what we expect, so that today it is almost impossible to see a living tissue in any other way than as an assembly of such sub-units. The word had not quite reached that point of dominance in Hooke's account[1]. He was still actively forming an interpretation, and not yet taking it for granted.

The acceptance of labelling in everyday life

In daily life we take a lot for granted, and use language in a labelling way all the time. In expressions like 'Pass the butter' or 'Turn the page' or 'Stir the water gently', we imagine quite reasonably that speaker and hearer are not in doubt about which substance is called 'the butter', or what actions 'turn' or 'stir' refer to. We can even be fairly sure what 'gently' indicates – or at least we can if we have not just come from teaching a group of eleven year olds how to 'stir gently'. I called the approach 'labelling', because it seems that the words correspond in a simple way to well-defined things, substances or actions. They seem like labels for those things, substances, or actions, and even for the adjectival or adverbial qualities which are ascribed to them.[2]

There is some truth in such a view, because language does make much use of arbitrary symbolisations. The word 'Whatsit' can in principle stand for any old 'thingemejig' if I choose to make it do so, and if my friends will accept it. If they do so, then I can show them how to fix the new whatsits to the other thingemejigs; they could ask me questions which I would understand, and we could soon have an extensive conversation on many aspects of whatsit-fixing and thingemejiggery. It would scarcely matter at all whether the initial use of 'Whatsit' emerged as an effort of interpretive figuration (like 'cell' did for Hooke). In principle, we might just as well agree to call it an 'X'. Thinking of this approach to language, all that matters is that a learner gets to use the right words – 'X', or 'Whatsit' – in the right context, and becomes able to pick out the thing, action or characteristic which corresponds to the word. Many people can identify the components of an electric circuit and wire it up quite successfully on the basis of just such familiarity with the language that labels its parts.

Interpreting and labelling: examples from the classroom

Even though arbitrariness does exist in language, when teachers use it interpretively they try to avoid that arbitrariness. They give, or look for, *reasons* why things are called in such and such a way. They signal in their own explanations that they are searching for an appropriate expression. They also expect their pupils to do the same, and encourage exploratory speech or writing from a learner. Between the lines the idea is communicated that there is more than one way to say something well, and language is not just a ready-made account of facts.

On the other hand, no teacher can be doing this all the time. We are often just familiarising learners with ready-made ways of talking, and so in a science teacher's language we find a mixture of the two approaches. For example, Janet – a teacher and a parent of many years' experience – often uses language in a clearly interpretive way, seeking to form and develop her own thoughts and those of her pupils by exploring ideas and puzzling them out with the help of words:

What's happening on this pond, then, when the insect skates about so lightly without falling through and getting wet? It's as if the surface were a kind of stretchy skin. Look carefully and you can see it dented where the legs are. Do you see what I mean?

or

If you were eating grass, like this sheep, you might need at least two kinds of teeth – sharp ones for cutting it off – and we call them cutters or 'incisors', and flatter ones for grinding it down to a pulp – I call them 'grinders'.

At other times what she says is much less exploratory, and more matter-of-fact. Her words then seem less for exploring ideas and more for describing facts and giving information:

Air contains mainly two gases – nitrogen and oxygen – and there is also some carbon dioxide, some water vapour, and some other gases.

That last sentence is almost entirely in the labelling style, and at one level it is quite acceptable teaching. Pupils can certainly take this information, get it down in notes, and make use of it later. But it gives no suggestion of a problem in understanding air, rather the opposite – it implies that air just *is*, and we can describe it in a certain way and no other. There is no hint that coming to a conclusion about what 'air' or 'airs' might be was a problem that absorbed the scientific community for the better part of a century. There is no acknowledgement that the word 'gas' was a triumph of theoretical insight, and no mention that arguments raged about whether it was a good idea to call 'lively air' by a new name: 'oxygen' (acid maker). The modern summary neglects to say that people wondered whether what we now label as nitrogen (nitre-maker) should be understood by calling it 'choking stuff' (*Stickstoff* in German) or 'lifeless' stuff (*Azote* in French). The results of all these efforts of thought are taken for granted, and their products are presented as labels for materials about whose existence we now feel confident. Overall, the modern statement about air appears like a description rather than an interpretation. It seems to consist of words which are just convenient names for the various components, no

more questionable than those in a statement such as 'This jam contains sugar, strawberries, and water'. Well of course they are convenient names, but they are also the products of interpretive effort.

Along the corridor, some of Janet's colleagues are altogether less tentative in presenting the results (and only the results) of scientific thought. They treat words nearly all the time as labels for things, rather than instruments of interpretation: **Atoms are made of protons, neutrons and electrons . . . The nucleus of each living cell contains chromosomes . . . Blood is expelled from the right ventricle along the pulmonary artery**. In this way some of the ideas of science get transformed into arbitrary information to be learned; they no longer retain the status of ideas at all, and scarcely seem to merit being puzzled over. If pupils are exposed to words in that way over and over again, they can get little sense of scientific language as an instrument of interpretation, and little incentive to use it themselves for sorting out the ideas.

From 'interpretation' to 'label' – a natural development in language

The transformation of consciously interpretive statements into something more literal is to some extent inevitable. By repetition, what starts as a 'manner of speaking' acquires a more taken-for-granted status, and it soon becomes in effect a set of labels. Science continuously generates new concepts by interpretive effort, and we immediately start to use them in new thoughts, and accept them as ordinary items to speak or write about. We try to make them retain a speculative status while we wait for evidence in support of their reasonableness, but there is also a familiarity effect and if their reasonableness is not denied, they gradually become real enough to be included in our accepted understanding of the world of nature. That change has gone further for 'genes', 'atoms' and 'electric currents' than it has for 'black holes'. Intangibles like 'electric current' and 'molecular orbitals' become altogether more substantial and thing-like in our minds. We could speak of this as the reification of concretisation of concepts, or as the literalisation of figurative language, instead of what I am calling it here, i.e. a process of allowing interpretations to take the status of labels.

I cannot argue that 'labels' should never be taught in school, because they are important products of scientific activity. Daily competence requires their use in that way, and it is certainly *part* of the job of a science teacher to build up familiarity with the account of the natural world as we currently understand it. What I do want to argue, however, is that habitual experience of labelling fosters a set of beliefs about language which can quickly de-skill the learners by cutting them off from the habit of re-processing ideas.

Two general conceptions of what language is

The left-hand column of the adjacent table sets out some of those beliefs. In summary we can say that when I am most steeped in labelling uses, language seems like just a commentary upon nature, and not like a means of deciding what nature is. The right-hand column of the table sets out a contrasting set of beliefs with more emphasis on the variability of words, the need to use them and talk round them to establish a meaning, and the importance of the learner's effort to re-process information. An individual teacher or pupil might be influenced by one or other of these approaches on different occasions, but it is easy to understand how in the context of science lessons the first view might come to predominate. Douglas Barnes called it a 'transmission' view, and found that it was more prevalent amongst science teachers than amongst teachers of the humanities.[3]

There is much in the culture of science to draw both teachers and learners towards such a view. Labelling language occurs over and over again as textbooks present modern descriptions of each topic with its modern technical terms. Expressions like 'I wonder, what did so-and-so have in mind when he wrote that sentence?' are not common and indeed they are thought by some to belong in lessons on English rather than lessons on science. On the grounds of familiarity alone we can see how

a general concept of language as a labelling system could grow up. In other parts of the curriculum where the question 'What can we take that statement to mean?' is more common, pupils and teachers might more easily develop a view of language as a system for interpreting and understanding.

More fundamentally it has been a hope and intention in science to try to make language into a straightforward description of things, with well-defined terms, and without vagueness. Thomas Sprat wrote of the early Fellows of the Royal Society that they were resolved

> **to return back to the primitive purity and shortness, when men delivered so many Things, almost in an equal number of words**.

Their successors have been extremely effective in talking about things and effects on things, mostly by devising new ways of doing so. They have produced huge numbers of new technical terms and made many airy abstractions like **forces** and **fields** so useful and so familiar that they can be treated in conversation just like real things.

As a result of all that effort words as used in science are very closely associated with the material world, and decidedly 'thing-ish', thus supporting the labelling view. They are rather precisely defined and are thought to be reliably unchanging in meaning. A good word in science is held to be one which has one meaning only, clear and unambiguous. Scientists and science teachers are aware that in other walks of life words are often ill-defined or used in many different ways, but those features are regarded as 'imperfections of language' – an unfortunate looseness practised by non-scientific people. William Whewell wrote in the 1830s:[4]

> **When our knowledge becomes perfectly exact and purely intellectual, we require a language which shall also be exact and intellectual; we shall exclude alike vagueness and fancy, imperfection and superfluity, in which each term shall convey a meaning steadily fixed and rigorously limited. Such is the language of science.**

Whether or not Whewell's prescription is valuable

Two conceptions of language		
	A view derived from frequent experience of language as a **labelling system**	A view derived from using it and hearing it used as an **interpretive system**
What language seems to do *vis-à-vis* the world of nature	Words correspond in a simple way to features of the external world.	Words highlight features to which we are attending, and so they steer thought and dialogue. Whether to call a lion a carnivore, a hunter or just a big cat is a speaker's decision in a particular context, not something dictated by the nature of the lion.
What the speaker thinks he or she is doing with language.	Describing, telling, reporting.	Figuring, exploring, teaching, persuading, suggesting.
How language is thought to work in scientific discovery	We find a fact and *then* find words to describe it.	We choose words which influence how we see the new point of interest, and how we can then talk about it.
How it is thought to work in communication generally	Like Morse Code in a wire, or packets in the post.	The important part is how you decode the Morse, or unpack the parcel and use the pieces it contains. What the hearer constructs may approximate to something like the speaker's intention, but communication is always partial.
How it is thought to work in learning	(i) Efficient clear transmission from teacher to learner is needed, and a learner must be a good receiver. (ii) The teacher's speech is very important	(i) The main process is the active interpretation and re-expression of ideas by the learner. (ii) The learner's speech is very important.
Assumptions about the **meanings of single words**	(i) They have a fixed meaning, at least for a particular context.	(i) Meanings vary from person to person as well as from context to context, and are influenced by a host of factors.
	(ii) A definition will capture the meaning.	(ii) Meanings are in minds rather than on paper, and even where definitions serve well there is always fuzziness at the edges, and that is an asset, not an imperfection.
Assumptions about the **meanings of extended statements**	If well stated these are unambiguous and clear to all.	(i) Such meanings are always debatable, and require an interpretive effort by the hearer or reader. (ii) Multiple meanings may be found in a single statement, and this is important, not an imperfection.

for the development of science, it is most unfortunate as regards the practice of education. It cuts us off from all those techniques which might otherwise invite the learner to consider just what a writer was trying to say. If the meaning of a scientific word, sentence, book, or theory is so clear and definite, what need is there to discuss it? We might just as well use the missile theory of communication – I launch the words, you catch them.

One's view of how language works can have a big influence on the amount of time made available for 'discussing and interpreting' as opposed to 'giving and receiving information', and indeed I suspect that the depth of conviction on this matter felt by a teacher or a pupil has more effect than available time or size of syllabus. Consequently from here onwards I want to show that scientific language is not as Whewell hoped, and the assumptions set out in the lower part of the left-hand column of the table of comparison are wrong. Scientific words and statements *do not* have simple fixed meanings, and hence to understand them it is necessary to employ interpretive learning and teaching techniques even though the product of learning is to include scientific language in its standard forms with precise, definite, economical statements.

A science teacher needs (as a scientist) to handle precision and also (as a teacher) to manage the exploration of ambiguity. I cannot do the second of these without moving freely amongst the ideas set out in the right-hand column of the table. When I understand that meaning is always liable to change, and variable from person to person, then I have a stronger rationale for helping learners to explore these variations and changes in their own thought.

Scorn for the labellers

To highlight the contrasts made so far, I shall end this chapter with a quotation from one extreme end of the spectrum of beliefs about language. In the humanities there are those who are much accustomed to using language in interpretive ways,

and very much less frequent users of it as a simple labelling system. They are extremely conscious of the inherent uncertainty in words, and the ease with which a slight difference in context or in emphasis can radically alter the meaning of what is said. For them there is no doubt that language is an interpretive medium. When it comes to communication, the idea that a good statement is one which says what it means and means what it says is a crude over-simplification. Some are deeply scornful of the kind of language to which science appears to aspire, and we can feel that scorn in Henry Reed's poem *Naming of Parts*. Different people will read the poem in different ways. Is it mainly about one man's response to military training, or mainly a scornful comment on a certain military 'cast of mind', or is it about the subtleties of language, or all of these? Anyway, where is 'the meaning' in the poem – on the lines, between the lines, or where? How do we 'get the meaning'? How many meanings are there? Reed's lines will provide me with a bridge to the next chapter, in which I want to write more about meaning in science, and about how learners are expected to 'get the meaning' of anything.

Notes

1 'Cells': The quotation is from Robert Hooke's *Micrographia* (1665) Observ. XVIII: 'Of the Schematisme or Texture of Cork and of the Cells and Pores of some other such frothy bodies', reprinted (1961) by Dover Publications, New York. In that particular account, Hooke seemed most interested in the overall texture of the material – its porosity, hole-iness, or frothiness, which would account for its lightness, its compressibility and its resilience when squeezed. He noted principally that '. . . it had very little solid substance in comparison with the empty cavity that was contained between'. The word 'cell' was not quite as central to his interpretation as it now appears to us in retrospect, when we think of it as a label for the units from which the material is built.

2 Labelling: My choice of the word 'labelling' for the most literalised language has parallels with its use in sociology. Labelling as a social phenomenon is associated with stereotyping – a 'working class person' or a 'troublemaker', or a 'chauvinist' and so on. Such

Naming of Parts

Today we have naming of parts. Yesterday,
We had daily cleaning. And tomorrow morning,
We shall have what to do after firing. But today,
Today we have naming of parts. Japonica
Glistens like coral in all of the neighbouring gardens,
And today we have naming of parts.

This is the lower sling swivel. And this
Is the upper sling swivel, whose use you will see,
When you are given your slings. And this is the piling swivel,
Which in your case you have not got. The branches
Hold in the gardens their silent, eloquent gestures,
Which in our case we have not got.

This is the safety-catch, which is always released
With an easy flick of the thumb. And please do not let me
See anyone using his finger. You can do it quite easy
If you have any strength in your thumb. The blossoms
Are fragile and motionless, never letting anyone see
Any of them using their finger.

And this you can see is the bolt. The purpose of this
Is to open the breech, as you see. We can slide it
Rapidly backwards and forwards: we call this
Easing the spring. And rapidly backwards and forwards
The early bees are assaulting and fumbling the flowers:
They call it easing the Spring.

They call it easing the Spring: it is perfectly easy
If you have any strength in your thumb: like the bolt,
And the breech, and the cocking-piece, and the point of balance,
Which in our case we have not got; and the almond-blossom
Silent in all of the gardens and bees going backwards and forwards,
For today we have naming of parts.

Henry Reed (1941)

Reprinted from Henry Reed's *Collected Poems* edited by Jon Stallworthy (1991) by permission of Oxford University Press.

labelling has been shown to generate expectations in the user which affect the interaction between the person who uses the label and the person(s) labelled. To give a classroom example, someone who labels a child as 'aggressive' may approach the child in a way that elicits the aggressive behaviour. Labelling limits the observer's perception to certain very restricted aspects of the person labelled. (See also my discussion of constructing and construing in Chapter 12.)

Just so in physical science (very usefully focusing attention on key features) and in teaching (not always so usefully). There is nothing wrong with allowing pupils to label something 'a Bunsen burner' once in a while, but to let them do so over and over again allows them to pigeon-hole it and stop looking at it, just as surely as any racist 'label' can cut off their attention to most of the human character of the person who is abused.

3 Transmission and Interpretation: This distinction was developed by Douglas Barnes in *From Communication to Curriculum*, Penguin, 1972. His emphasis was on interpretation by the pupil, and he was especially interested in the proportion of lesson time devoted to it, as well as in the amount of freedom allowed for pupils to explore around a topic as opposed to getting directly to the statement of public knowledge which is the goal the 'transmissive' teacher has very sharply in mind. The working out of this distinction resulted in the publication of many books on language 'across the curriculum', e.g. C. R. Sutton (ed.) (1991) *Communicating in the Classroom*, Hodder and Stoughton, 10th impression. Douglas Barnes later extended his enquiry into the nature and purposes of writing in the secondary school: see Yanina Sheeran and Douglas Barnes (1991) *School Writing*, Open University Press.

4 Scientific meaning 'steadily fixed and rigorously limited'. The quotation is from William Whewell (1840) *The Philosophy of the Inductive Sciences*, recounted by T. H. Savory (1953) in *The Language of Science*, Deutsch. Savory points out that the effort to sustain a fixed meaning for a scientific word involves repelling peripheral associations from which a shift in meaning could begin, a feature to be discussed in Chapter 8.

Variation and change in meaning

Immersion in the culture of science draws my attention away from variability of meaning, and leaves me with an implicit assumption that people's interpretations of words and sentences will be uniform. **Metals are shiny** . . . **Acids contain hydrogen** . . . **Water boils at 100° C** . . . Should I stop and think that others may not visualise quite what I do when the word 'metal' is spoken, or that their idea of an 'acid' or even 'water' may be very different from my own? All these words are very definite in science and my expectation is that someone will either understand the scientific meaning or will not do so, in which case I could explain. My first inclination in teaching is to focus just on the new and special words which I believe may be strange to the pupils. If I say **'Water is a compound of hydrogen and oxygen'** I would explain 'compound' but not worry much about 'water'. Similarly, I might not bother much about 'metal' and 'boil', unless they were the focus of the lesson, and if any doubt should emerge later it would be easy to show how they are defined, and replace the 'incorrect' meanings with the 'correct' scientific ones. I certainly do not expect to look into *shades* of meaning in these words.

Unfortunately, however, *shades* of meaning are very important in any *new* thought. A shift of attention from one shade of meaning to another is what initiates a new understanding.[1] In my role as a teacher I really want to see such changes of understanding, and so I need something to pull my attention towards the differences, some way of making them more explicit.

The influence of context

To 'get the meaning' of anything – whether it be a poem or a scientific statement – you do not listen only to the individual words. You comprehend them by awareness of the setting or context in which they occur – and that includes the sentence, the topic, the place, who is speaking, and even the intonation which the speaker uses. **'Now let's look at the cells'** may seem uncomplicated when we hear it from a teacher standing by a microprojector, but suppose that we hear it again next day on a visit to a police station? The different context would drag what appears to be one word – cells – into an almost totally different set of connections. People are inclined to say 'Ah, we just have two different meanings here – the scientific one and the everyday one', but I see it as just a very big shift of attention amongst all one's possible mental states of attention. Perhaps a meaning is just a particular set of connections, elicited by a particular context. What meaning you get depends on which connections you are attending to.[2]

Word meanings: core and periphery

To make sense of differences of understanding, both large and small, we need to trace the connections which people are making, and for that purpose it is useful to distinguish two different components or aspects of a word's meaning:

(i) the 'logical', 'conceptual' or 'denotative' limits of the word, expressed in its main logical connections, and

(ii) a variety of extra associations and connections to other experience, especially extra connotations from past use, and affective overtones.

The best available shorthand is to call them the **denotative** and **associative** components.[3] We can also think of them as a **core** of essentials, and a **periphery** through which the word connects in many different ways to the rest of a person's understanding. For **water**, to express the core we could speak of 'a liquid which freezes at $0°$ C and boils at $100°$ C', or perhaps of 'a compound of hydrogen and oxygen', but the periphery will include a myriad of associations. Some, like fluidity and wetness, might be similar for everyone, but other more strongly emotional associations could be very different from person to person – the pleasure of cool streams, or the fear of drowning. These have traditionally been rejected as not relevant to the scientific consideration of water. The periphery however is more important than is commonly recognised, for two main reasons. Firstly the peripheral connections give reality to the idea, so that the word has both logical and emotional depth to it, and is more than an empty verbalism. Secondly, it is from shifts of attention and other changes within the periphery that new understanding comes.

Change in the core

For **metal** we could try to agree the core meaning as (say) a type of material with certain properties such as electrical conductivity, etc. What is in the periphery will vary according to the range of one's acquaintance with metals, as for instance when a child describes metals as 'hard', which is true for some but not all metals. That example shows how the core itself will change when the user of the word can draw on more instances of its use. A classificatory definition of a metal as a hard shiny substance is reasonable on the basis of experience of iron, steel and brass objects; it can be a kind of core meaning for you, even though it is not the accepted public one. Further experience with lead, lithium, and other metals will eventually change that understanding.

For **acid** the core may once have been represented by a phrase such as 'a sour substance', but nowadays, and for a scientist, it involves 'containing replaceable hydrogen' or 'capable of yielding hydrogen ions'. The periphery could include features which are true of all acids but seem more or less prominent to different people, such as 'will turn litmus red' or 'is an electrolyte'. It may also include associations such as 'dangerous' which are an outstanding feature of how one person understands an acid, but which are not true of all acids and must certainly be excluded from the core. Again, we see that what is accepted as the core meaning is itself subject to change.

In developing successively more refined versions of a core, one approach is to regard the word as associated not actually with the tangible metal or acid, but with a general concept or categorisation abstracted from the experience of many examples. The word **acid** summons up what acids have in common, just as 'red' summons up what red things have in common. This view leads directly into a teaching method which presents example after example in order to get over the idea. 'Here is an acid and here is another – see this, try this, notice what they have in common.' A definition does not come early in such a teaching sequence, but it may be used later as a summary after considerable practical experience, and then again after a search for an underlying explanation of the similarities. The *classificational* definition is gradually supplemented or replaced by a more *theoretical* one. 'A sour substance' gives way to 'a substance containing replaceable hydrogen'. A list of characteristic features of metals gives way to a summary of the kind of atomic structure which makes them metallic. A **force** might be introduced as a classificatory name for all sorts of pushes and pulls, but eventually it will be defined in a more theoretical way, in relation to other key terms.

The refinement of these core meanings is a very important part of science, and the main point of this chapter is to show that they are not independent of what is going on in the periphery.

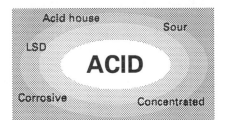

Some possible words in the partial shadow when one's attention is called to 'Acid'

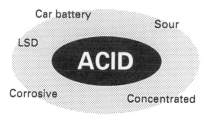

Viewing the 'penumbra of meaning' the other way around

Systems of notation?

No really satisfactory system of notation exists to express the relationship between the above components of meaning, but we can try to show it visually in several ways. One is to sketch the word inside an area of bright illumination with semi-illumination around it. As we momentarily direct our attention to a word, what else do we see out of the corner of our mind's eye, which might set us on a train of connections to other words and ideas? Several writers have had some version of this image in mind when speaking of the 'penumbra' of meaning around a word – the area of partial shadow which grades off into obscurity, as shown in the diagram (left) above. The phrase 'penumbra of meaning' is attributed to an English scholar,[4] but it may have some appeal to scientists. Those who are accustomed to textbook diagrams of eclipses may think of penumbra the other way round (right diagram) – a gradation from very dark to very light!

The most important feature of this representation is the *indefiniteness* away from the centre. It is not possible to say exactly what falls within the peripheral area, or what may do so in future. In the partial shadow, before we organise our thoughts in a logical manner, there may be all sorts of other trigger words for other areas of meaning – as shown above by the inclusion of words from the world of drugs. It would be silly to claim that these are completely irrelevant to the meanings of the word 'acid', if they are actually elicited by it. On the other hand, they may fade into unimportance as we firm up those which are important for the scientific uses of the word. Extending the illumination metaphor, what falls within the penumbra can be changed by altering the direction of illumination. That is what a teacher can do, steering attention towards some of the existing associations rather than others.

Slightly more convenient on paper is the 'burr notation'.[5] It shows a central area surrounded in two or three dimensions with hooks that grapple other words. The term is derived from the name of the fruits of plants such as the burdock, where dispersal is achieved by means of hundreds of hooklets which can tangle in the wool of passing animals. Words are thought to have a potential for logical or illogical mental connection to any of hundreds of other words, and the diagrams show them 'hooking on' to these others so that we can explore chains and networks of interconnected thought. The diagrams do not necessarily imply a behaviourist mechanism for word association; indeed they relate more closely to attempts at 'cognitive mapping' of an overall structure of thought.[5]

Each hook makes a connection with another word which could itself be the centre of a burr, and so on through chains and webs of interconnection. Gaining more connections represents an enrichment of meaning, and selecting some rather than others initiates the development of a specialised meaning in a particular context.

It is very difficult to capture on paper what one might imagine is going on in someone's head in a more fluid and dynamic fashion, but this notation has several strengths as an aid to thinking about the effects of a word on someone who hears it. It shows how a word with few connections could be relatively meaningless until some are established, but on the other hand it does not quite succeed in showing how the formation of a linkage subtly changes the words which are linked. The hooks catch associations of several different kinds – examples, characteristics, feelings, logical contrasts and so on, which are not totally independent. To see and handle citric acid and aspirin in the context of a discussion of acids would increase the number of hooks to examples but cause other associations – such as those to 'liquid' and to 'dangerous' – to fade away. On a plant burr, all hooks are of similar status, but in the 'burr diagrams' of words it has yet to be determined

whether different strengths of attachment or different kinds of relationship should be shown by different kinds of hook. *Perhaps the core meaning is better represented by a cluster of the most important connections.* I shall try to use that approach, and show some hooks in my diagrams as thicker than others.

Charting changes in meaning for a learner

Although the burr notation cannot cope with all the subtleties of meaning change, it is nevertheless a useful device to start a discussion of those changes, and we can use it to explore how meanings might change over time. Reworking some of the examples already discussed, here are some possible changes over time in an individual pupil.

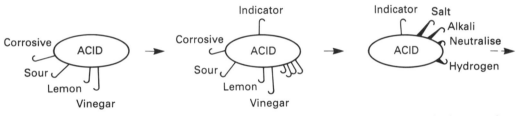

For ACID, the left-hand burr represents some part of the understanding of a young learner who has very few associations to the word, and an ill-defined core. At the second stage, school experience has increased the number of examples (as shown by more hooks shown at the bottom right, to hydrochloric, nitric, and other acids), and it has also drawn out carefully what they have in common, to the point where the core could be a temporary classificational 'definition', e.g. a substance which turns litmus red. At the third stage, use of the word during activities chosen to emphasise the reaction of acids with metals to yield hydrogen, leads to a different way of delimiting the core, and a stronger bond to the words 'hydrogen', 'salt', 'alkali' and 'neutralise'. Later stages will make, and then emphasise, connections to the vocabulary of electrical conductivity and ionisation.

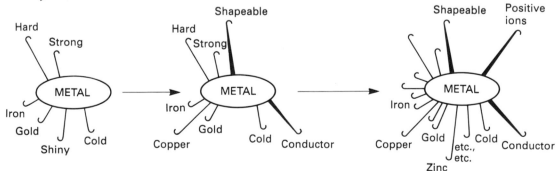

For METAL, the development again starts with more examples, then drawing out key properties, and eventually a change in the relative importance of different connections.

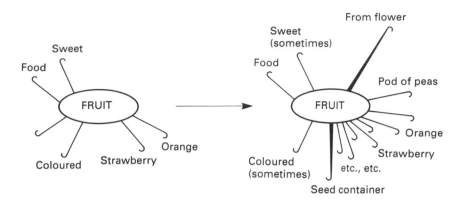

For FRUIT, the strongest connections in an early understanding may be to sweet foods. Extra exemplars lead to a shift of emphasis amongst different attributes and so to the biologist's meaning, with its crucial connection to 'seed container'.

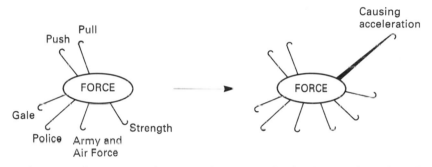

FORCE has a very rich variety of associations from everyday uses, and only a few are shown here. It is tempting simply to reject all these and focus on one new defining feature.

Many teachers work by drawing out existing associations, and gradually changing the emphasis and their relative importance, but in science it is all too easy simply to reject the unwanted associations as 'wrong' and to imply that the *real* meaning is the scientific one. Burr diagrams can help to alert both learner and teacher to the range of existing connections, how they are changing, and which ones apply in which context. They might also help to ensure that older connections are not entirely shut off from those in science, with the scientific way of talking totally isolated from everything else that the learner understands.

Charting changes in the public meaning of scientific words

We can also use the burr notation to chart changes in the meanings of words as accepted in the community of scientists. Consider for example the successive meanings of **element**, and particularly **chemical element** as understood in 1670, 1790 and 1930. In the first phase, Boyle had started to reject the traditional 'four elements' of earth, air, fire and water (more like four qualities contributing to the nature of things), and similarly to reject other alchemical 'principles' such as 'sulphur' (better

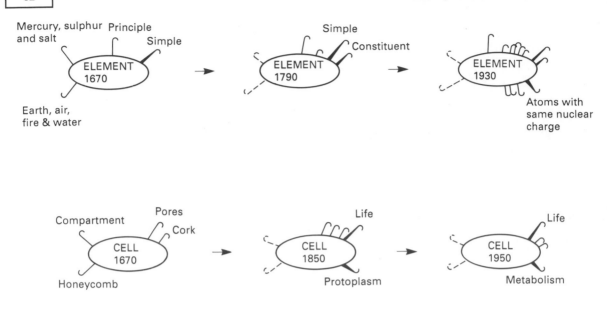

rendered now as the 'sulphurousness' of some things). He was starting instead to associate the word **element** with something more definitely material – a 'perfectly unmingled substance'. In the second phase, Lavoisier was determined to concentrate on the constituent substances from which more complicated ones are built, and he constructed a list of such 'simple bodies', but still included the 'imponderable' ('unweighable') **light** and **caloric**. Within a few decades after that, the scientific community had taken his reasoning further and accepted that 'substantial' in its scientific sense required that any **'substance'** must be weighable, and so light and caloric were rejected from the later lists. By 1930 the concept of atomic number had become the theoretical basis of what 'element' means to a scientist, and the discovery of isotopes had reversed an earlier trend and allowed one to think of an element as actually a mixture.

Throughout this period the word element continued to be used in other contexts, as when we speak of the elements of geometry, or an element in the argument, and other more specific uses continue to emerge, as when we speak of the heating element in a kettle. All the corresponding associations can be part of its live meaning today, some of them influencing the scientific sense, and

some possibly distracting a learner. Burrs could be used to show a radiation of several meanings from an earlier point of divergence, but in the following selection just the one chemical line of development is shown. The diagrams include just a few of the relevant associations. The oldest, which in this case appear on the extreme left, can be thought of as associations which are markedly weakened but perhaps not entirely lost.

Similarly we can look at the changing associations to the word **cell** in biology. First there was its transfer from the generality of 'compartment' or the specificity of the honeycomb, when it was re-applied to something under the microscope. Later it came to be understood as an important and general unit of life, full of **protoplasm**, and later still as a complex of interlocking chemical reactions, so that the word in its scientific meaning now has strong connections to other new words such as **metabolism**. Again here are just a few of the relevant associations.

Readers might like to try similar diagrams to show the changing meanings of **air** – prior to its being thought of as a chemical mixture, then during the eighteenth century when various different 'airs' were being identified, and finally after the establishment of the oxygen theory of combustion.

I have included these accounts of historical change simply to emphasise that even the accepted public meanings in science are not as fixed as we might hope. Scientific words (and symbols[6]) are subject to the processes of change, development and decay, just as in any other area of language. We try to slow up the process by defining and delimiting them, but new experimental investigations cause shifts in one's attention to different parts of the periphery of the words one is using. Different features assume greater or lesser importance, and the meaning is altered. T. S. Kuhn has pointed out that after crucial periods of change in thought ('scientific revolutions'), the important words get new meanings within the new matrix of thought.

It can be argued that professional training of scientists requires a somewhat uncritical acceptance of the new meaning within the new thought-system. If so, using language as if it were a 'labelling' system, as discussed in the previous chapter, may be a way of achieving that training. I find it hard to agree however that in any educational context one is justified in teaching the current specialist meaning as the only possible one. To re-emphasise the contrast of assumptions about word meanings, I summarise below part of the table from the previous chapter.

The importance of peripheral aspects of meaning to a learner

The particular associations in an *individual's* periphery of meaning matter to that individual not only because they connect it up and make it usable in relation to other thoughts, but also because they are personal to that individual. A word, by having these associations, can become a possession – a part of that person's competence, not just something belonging to the teacher and textbook writer.

School science has long been open to the criticism that some pupils leave school unskilled at using scientific ideas in everyday contexts, and more recently it has also been blamed for not overcoming the image of science as cold, impersonal, clinical, unfriendly, and not of personal concern to the average teenager. The most successful learners may never have had those problems, but insofar as others do we should seek possible causes. The habit of isolating a core meaning and neglecting to explore the periphery cannot have helped.

Before attempting a remedy along the lines suggested here, we should perhaps acknowledge that the habit of trying to isolate and insulate core meanings was developed for what seemed like

Assumptions about the meanings of words	
as **LABELS**	as a means of **INTERPRETATION**
(i) They have a fixed meaning, at least for a particular context.	(i) Meanings vary from person to person as well as from context to context, and are influenced by a host of factors.
(ii) A definition will capture the meaning.	(ii) Meanings are in minds rather than on paper, and even where definitions serve well there is always fuzziness at the edges, and that is an asset, not an imperfection.

good reasons – i.e. to prevent misunderstandings and confusions! If you generate new thoughts in the course of your science, you can try to express them by 'stealing' existing words and using them in a new way which eventually necessitates a redefinition, or you may invent new words to avoid misunderstanding. Both approaches have been common, and both involve a neglect of the periphery. As an example of the first approach, **alive** is an existing word taken over by biologists. It acquires a technical meaning which is maintained by ceasing to attend to the earlier connotations of 'liveliness', 'vivacity' or 'quickening'. Concentrating on its biological meaning, one may be mildly surprised when a child classifies a flame as 'alive'. The second approach involves a more calculated insulation from anything people might have in mind beforehand. You form a new word using Greek or Latin components – **amorphous** rather than 'shapeless', **hypogeal** rather than 'underground', **herbicide** rather than 'plant-killer'. The new word can stand for something cleanly technical, without carrying over unwanted associations, especially unwanted emotional associations. In the process there is a gain in setting the context and specialist meaning, but a loss if the learner is deprived both of the thought sequence which led to the word, and of its wider connections. Clearly there is a danger,

to say the least, that the scientific habit of cutting off the emotional connotations is counter-productive in education if it makes science seem inhuman and unfriendly *and* takes away the means of clothing words with some reality. Even if the isolation mechanisms are appropriate for science, they are much less so for general education.

One advantage of words from a dead language, however, is that a teacher can take a middle path by translating them to give the wider sense of understanding, and then using them, sure that there will not be confusion with everyday uses. Bigger problems arise when the scientific topic has not got its own new words. The scientific statements then assault the learners, and threaten to make them deny their commonsense understanding of the language. Words in danger of doing this include **reduce** and **reduction** in chemistry and **force, pressure, weight, work** and **power** in physics. They are all used just as frequently outside science as inside it, and it is anti-educational to imply, however unintendedly, that the non-scientific meanings are somehow weak. In the following panel, a biology teacher (who was in other ways very proud of scientific language) uses his pen to berate his physics colleagues on this point, perhaps slightly tongue-in-cheek.

A biologist is unkind about the language habits of his colleagues . . .

'The mathematical physicist is guilty of linguistic rape of a family of related words – force, work, power and weight. In mechanics, force does not mean strength, as it does when the ordinary man says that he is perhaps impressed by the force of an argument. It is given a rather precise and intricate definition . . . quite different from anything that the word force implies in everyday life. . . . A weight, one is surprised to learn, is not . . . the familiar block of metal with a ring on the top . . . the weight of a thing has to be the force with which the earth attracts it. Work gives even more trouble, because a physicist has decided that a force works, or does work, only when it moves something. I may push and pull in vain at an immovable object, make myself hot and tired by my efforts, and find that mathematically I have done no work. But if I seize the dangling reins of a runaway horse and pull them, and find that nevertheless the animal continues on its course, I have had work done on me, and I, panting and dishevelled, have done less than no work. After this it is quite easy to accept the idea that power has come to mean the rate at which work can be done . . .'

T. H. Savory (1959) in *The Language of Science*

A clash in the meanings of 'conservation'

This problem, of the science teacher seeming to reject the learner's intelligence, is particularly acute today in connection with the words **conserve** and **conservation** in relation to **energy**. Much has been written about energy, so let me come at it another way by considering the periphery of **conserve**. This word is actively in use in the community at large, and it has very long-established meanings concerned with protecting, saving, and keeping from decay and wastage. Fisheries and water resources are to be conserved, and organisations called conservancies have existed for that purpose for centuries. Ancient documents and paintings in danger of disintegration are handed to conservators, and buildings are conserved against dilapidation. Fruit is conserved as jam. Even without its connections to 'conservative' these uses give a clear meaning of conserve as a process of protection against loss, wastage and disintegration. Topical talk about conserving forests and endangered species has strengthened that meaning in recent years. We have a Nature Conservancy Council, environmental conservation campaigns, and drives which urge us to undertake fuel conservation. Since fuel has something to do with energy, it is understandable that what might be best expressed as **Conserve Fuel** is often rendered as **Conserve Energy**. That phrase has a real meaning for people, even though within it the word written as **E-n-e-r-g-y** means more what a scientist could call **'available-energy'** – stored, usable, useful, accessible. That is what needs protecting.

An approach to teaching which respects the learner's intuitions from life experience would begin with this understanding, and not attempt to deny it. We can support the idea of available, usable, useful, accessible or organised energy, and say: 'A fuel (with some air to burn it) is very useful to us as a kind of store. Don't let the *available energy* of the fuel–air system run to randomised waste, heating up the atmosphere, because in that state it will no longer be of use to us.'

In practice, a pair of different meanings, which seem to contradict everything that the government's 'Department of Energy' is urging, are pushed forward. Energy cannot be destroyed, it says in the science course; it is already conserved! Whatever this physicist's 'conserve' means, it is not the meaning described above, and whatever this 'energy' is, it is certainly not what the young citizen expects. Nor is it 'vigour' or 'health' or any of the other everyday meanings.

What seems to have happened historically is that a very specialised variant in the meaning of **conserve** came to appeal to the scientific community, and it helped people to check for something that is the same before and after various changes. If so much fuel is burned in the steam engine, then in principle so much water could be lifted from the mineshaft with a pump. If so much motion is randomised, so much heating effect will be observed. Such and such electrical activity will bring about the same heating effect, and so on. Several words and phrases were influential as people tried to decide the nature of this whatever-it-is that stays the same. They included 'force', 'strength', 'living force' and its 'mechanical effect',

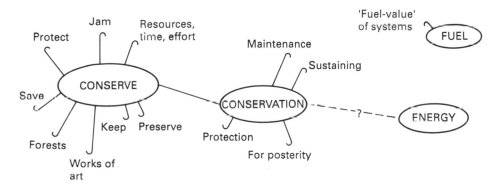

'living force' contrasted with 'tensional force', and so on. Eventually 'energy' emerged as the preferred term, within a new scheme of thought. There was perhaps some relief that other words (especially 'force') could be left behind, or confined to other uses. Joule's words show us an interesting stage in the development of ways of talking about this topic.[7]

Conserve in the sense demanded by the First Law of Thermodynamics is a term of accountancy, mathematics and logic. What is the same before and after some change? What equates? That is what we say is 'conserved'. Such a use had already got into science before the development of the idea of energy. It was in 'conservation of momentum' before and after collisions, and in 'conservation of weighable matter' before and after a chemical reaction. In this century it has been used in Piaget's child development studies – conservation of number before and after you give out your sweets, and of volume before and after you pour out the milk into separate glasses. However, it is not the common meaning intended in 'Conserve our stocks of coal and oil'. For this reason, some teachers[8] now suggest that the topic should *begin* with the Second Law of Thermodynamics, expressed in a form such as '**Available or usable energy** is easily redistributed into an unusable state'. This acknowledges the everyday understanding, but renders it in a way which can lead on eventually to the scientific meaning of **energy** and of the expression '**not lost or gained**', when the need arises for the physicist's techniques of accountancy. It may therefore be a better starting point in a spiral curriculum, where this particular strand is bound to be revisited many times.

Journeys in thought

The peripheral aspects of meaning should be an important object of study for teachers and learners, because of the potential they contain for the development of new meanings. Active learners are experiencing meaning-shift all the time, and if we have some simple techniques for encouraging them to explore the periphery of their own thought

we can help them to know directly how language is used as an interpretive system. They may then glimpse some of the great journeys in thought that were accomplished by that means, and which led to the formation of the major scientific concepts, and we can perhaps accompany them on a journey which covers some of the same terrain.[9]

The labelling and interpretive views of language have very different consequences for teachers. One relies on trying to pass on ready-made meanings 'directly'. The other requires careful exploration of the areas of uncertainty, with the teacher as a sort of coach, encouraging successive adjustments of understanding. For a teacher to occupy that coaching role, he or she needs to retain a sense of the interpretive function of scientific language, and also to know something of how the major concepts were developed. These conditions are not easily met if one's own professional education as a science graduate contained years of using language in its labelling forms. The journey to our present concepts has perhaps been forgotten,[10] and the habit of taking them for granted will need to be overcome. Otherwise we shall succumb repeatedly to long-standing pressures of time and content. For surely there is the syllabus, and today we must have the naming of parts.

Notes

1 Attention to shades of meaning as the origin of new thought: This idea underpins most of the literature on metaphor which I surveyed in the notes to Chapter 3. It was also very well expressed by Jacob Bronowski (1966) in an essay comparing creativity in science with creativity in literature. See 'The logic of the mind' in Bronowski's collected essays entitled *A Sense of the Future*, M.I.T. Press, 1977.

> . . . progress from the present account (of nature) to the next account is made by the exploration of ambiguities in the language that we use at this moment. In science these ambiguities are resolved for the time being, and a system without ambiguity is built up provisionally, until it is shown to fall short.

School pupils too are progressing from their 'present account' to the next one.

2 Changes of context do not simply switch us from one fixed meaning to another fixed meaning. Since no two contexts are ever exactly the same, and words themselves form part of the context in which other words occur, it can be argued that no word ever has exactly the same meaning twice. See S. I. Hayakawa and A. R. Hayakawa (1990) *Language in Thought and Action* (5th edn.) Harvard University Press, p. 39. On this view, communication depends not on arguing about what the 'real' meaning is, but on building up enough similarity of context for speaker and hearer to make many of the same connections to the word in question.

3 Components of meaning: Geoffrey Leech (1974) lists seven 'types of meaning' or aspects which contribute to the communicative effect of what is said. My simplification to two components is a derivative of his system. See Geoffrey Leech (1974) *Semantics*, Pelican Books. In marking off a denotative core from a periphery of sundry associations, I also have in mind the tension that exists between efforts to limit the meanings of words and efforts to explore the total range of their effects. The vocabulary of such efforts is itself of interest:

  (i) When we try to set the limits of words we talk about what they denote, designate, signify or refer to. We try to *define, determine and specify* their limits. We use them to *distinguish and differentiate* one category from another.

  (ii) On the other hand, when we attend to the unlimited aspects of words we talk of what they *imply, suggest or convey*, and of what they *elicit or evoke* in the hearer.

4 Penumbra of meaning – the partial shadows: T. H. Savory in *The Language of Science*, Deutsch (1953) attributes this phrase to Professor Simeon Potter, author of *Our Language*, Penguin (1950). Our commonest phrase for subtle variation and uncertainty is 'shades of meaning' and this may also be partly inspired by the idea of gradualness of change that one sees in a zone of partial light. More likely it is from the similar gradation one can achieve with a pencil or a paintbrush. The word 'nuance' from French has a similar origin.

5 Burr diagrams. For various forms of this notation see: (i) Tony Buzan (1974) *Use your Head*, BBC Books; (ii) Gerhard Schaefer (1979) 'Concept formation in biology', *European Journal of Science Education*, **1**, pp. 87–101; (iii) C. R. Sutton (1980) 'Science, language and meaning', *School Science Review*, **62**, pp. 47–56.

In the forms used so far, a hook can attach to almost any other word or phrase and its value is just to alert us to the fact that there is some connection. On the end of the hook we might have an established extra connotation of the stimulus word, or the name of an example, or a logical contrast, or a word which describes its affective tone, or just a chance word which is habitually linked for reasons which the hearer does not understand. As I explain in the main text, the various kinds of connection affect each other and the core. More examples lead to the formation of alternative lists of important attributes, and in some cases a new classificational definition can be built from these attributes to form a new core meaning. It seems unlikely that the notation can be improved to show all these effects. Hence it will probably remain a teaching tool rather than a research tool, a useful device for starting a discussion of meanings and changes in meaning, not a fully systematic way of describing them.

There are, however, some related questions for research, such as the effect that a context can have in apparently blocking off some potential connections. There is something about the organisation of semantic memory which exerts such a blocking effect. If I hear the word 'solution' in connection with salt and water, the connections to 'dissolve' and 'mix' are activated, but only with some difficulty do I recover other connections to 'problem', 'answer' and 'mathematics'. That is one of the difficulties which beset attempts to extend the burr diagrams into some form of 'cognitive map' of a person's understanding. Nevertheless, the burr notation does invite thought about a map of meaningful connections – a map constantly being redrawn perhaps. The most extended exploration of this topic as it applies in science education has been made by J. D. Novak. Without Novak's efforts, the writings of David Ausubel on meaningful verbal learning might not have reached the attention of science teachers. See: (i) D. P. Ausubel (1963) *The Psychology of Meaningful Verbal Learning*, Grune and Stratton, New York; (ii) D. P. Ausubel, J. D. Novak and H. Hanesian (1978) *Educational Psychology: A cognitive view*, 2nd edn., Holt, Rinehart and Winston; and (iii) J. D. Novak and D. B. Gowin (1984) *Learning How to Learn*, Cambridge University Press.

6 Shifts of emphasis affecting symbols as well as words. A salt which would once have been written $CuO.SO_3$ to show its relation to an acidic oxide and a basic

oxide, is now written $CuSO_4$ in response to an ionic theory of its structure.

7 Conserve, conservancy, conservation: For an historical account of the development of the specialist meaning of conserve in relation to the First Law, see Charles Singer (1959) in *A Short History of Scientific Ideas*, Oxford University Press, and P. M. Harman (1982) *Energy Force and Matter – The conceptual development of nineteenth century physics*, Cambridge University Press. Singer, interestingly, writes about this period under the heading 'Doctrine of Energy'. Joule's 1847 lecture in Manchester was one of the key events in the story, and it contained the following phrasing, as Joule talked around the idea of non-destruction, and showed his own confidence in the newly-realised mechanico-thermal equivalence.

> Living force (vis viva) is one of the most important qualities with which matter can be endowed, and as such it would be absurd to imagine that it can be destroyed. . . . Experiment has shown that wherever living force is apparently destroyed, whether by percussion, friction or any similar means, an exact equivalent of heat is restored. The converse is also true, namely that heat cannot be lessened or absorbed without the production of living force or its equivalent attraction through space. . . . Heat, living force and attraction through space . . . are mutually convertible. In these conversions nothing is ever lost.

Soon after this, William Thomson, sensing a contradiction between Joule's assertions, and earlier ideas about the non-destruction of 'heat' (i.e. the supposed fluid called caloric), began the task of reconciling the two systems. He used the word energy during those efforts, and eventually he and Clausius and others unified the system which we now call Thermodynamics. It is within that system, and only within that system, that the word 'energy' gets its specialist meaning. Joule's choice of words, made prior to that unification, retains much influence. It still echoes through the school-rooms, and not always with happy effects. For example 'conversion' easily leads on to 'into different forms', and some modern teachers find that embarrassing, because they do not want to suggest that energy is any kind of stuff; they want people to think of it as a property of a system. Clearly there is a tangle of different ways of talking even amongst scientists and teachers. Meanwhile the

general citizenry has got hold of the word energy and by usage it has acquired a meaning that fits the citizen's meaning of conserve.

The present impasse in teaching this topic will not be resolved until teachers can accept more unreservedly the citizen's meanings of Energy and Conserve, and then find ways to show how the specialist meanings of 'energy' and 'conserve' connect with them. The studies mentioned in Note 8 prepare the way for such an approach. The citizen's meanings have become increasingly well established in recent years as a result of public concern over the environment, and science teachers will have to accommodate to that situation. Shifts of meaning are a fact of life; language changes, and 'you can't buck the language' indefinitely.

8 The Second Law first, i.e. teaching 'energy spreading' before 'energy accounting': See Keith Ross (1988) 'Matter scatter and energy anarchy – The second law of thermodynamics is simply common experience', *School Science Review*, **69**, pp. 438–45. For an enquiry into children's understandings of 'conservation', see E. Boyes and M. Stanisstreet (1990), *School Science Review*, **72**, pp. 51–8. Both papers refer to earlier discussions of the problem by Joan Solomon and by Jon Ogborn.

A significant aspect of this approach is the teacher's effort to make more use of the terms 'fuel' and 'fuel value' in early teaching, for that which needs protecting, and which can be used up.

9 Journeys in thought: See Rosalind Driver (1976) 'Science – A journey in thought' in *Non-streamed Science and the Training of Teachers*, Association for Science Education, Hatfield. That account was mainly about the time needed to help pupils who are 'treading the path between everyday language . . . and the specialist language of science', and the kinds of talk in the classroom which it needs. I am using the phrase to show the relationship between that and the similar path trodden by scientists.

10 Recovering the older journeys in thought: Since many modern degree courses in science do not include the history of ideas, how can a science teacher get to know more about how concepts were developed? Within the rationale of this book, that is certainly an important part of one's professional preparation. Biographies of individual scientists are often helpful, and for a general overview, there are some older books which have proved their worth, for example Charles Singer's *A Short History of Scientific Ideas*, referred to in Note 7 above, and A. E. E.

McKenzie (1960) *The Major Achievements of Science*, Cambridge University Press. A starting point on individual scientific topics can often be found in W. F. Bynum, E. J. Browne and R. Porter (eds) (1981) *Dictionary of the History of Science*, published by Macmillan. A commentary on a wide range of resources is given by Stephen Pumphrey (1991) in 'History of science in the national curriculum: a critical review of resources and their aims', *British Journal for the History of Science,* **24**, pp. 61–78.

CHAPTER 9

Well, Mary, what are they saying here?

What are the consequences for the classroom of the account of scientific language which I have given? I have stressed the variability of meaning, its changes over time, and the value of exploring such changes with learners. I have also tried to show the value of recognising language as an interpretive system rather than a set of labels, and in taking that view, I forsake one of the major traditions of science teaching – that ideas emerge from 'seeing what happens' in experiments. The consequences are therefore not small. It is not a matter of adding a language-based activity here and there, but rather of shifting one's stance about what scientific knowledge is, and about how we engage the learner's involvement in a science lesson.

I should say here that the prospect of *adding* anything to an already crowded agenda for science is something I would want to resist, so in seeking to outline the day-to-day implications of my position I am also considering how the modern goals of school science might be achieved more effectively, more efficiently, and with greater satisfaction to pupils and teachers. I therefore want to explore the balance amongst the various activities that can go on in science lessons. How much telling? How much 'doing'? How much puzzling and problem solving? As I see it, good telling and good puzzling can both gain greater prominence, while 'doing' should be derived from these and made more purposeful by that connection, and less time-consuming.

I am sure that if learners are to get a feel for language as an interpretive system, they must have experience of using it that way themselves. They should also regularly meet scientific ideas which are presented as expressions of thought rather than definite information, so that there is some point in puzzling over them. Most important, a reasonable proportion of the lesson time should be devoted to comparing different people's understanding. The phrasing in the title of this chapter is meant to point in that direction. There is an explanation of some scientific idea, probably on paper. The teacher signals that there is room for doubt about it, provides space for the pupil to make an interpretation, and tries to maintain a relationship which can carry discussion. Many teachers work this way intuitively in their informal interactions with pupils, but my contention is that the established routines of science lessons do not make adequate provision for it in the formal business of the lesson.

Puzzling and telling are complementary. A clear exposition by the teacher, or in the pages of a book, is one component, but the pupils' learning is in making sense of what is said or written. Lessons organised with this in mind should therefore include time for puzzling, and for pupils to restate what they understand to be the key ideas. Although this sometimes occurs informally in discussion, it will normally require some structure, and some formal means of public report about what they have made of the topic.

In practice, tasks of that kind are not given substantial periods of time, however much their use has been urged. There is something in the traditions of science teaching which marginalises them, and can even make them unsuccessful when first tried. It is partly the pupils' own expectations of language – i.e. of *not* using it to explore and interpret ideas, or at least not doing so in science. It is also an over-confidence in practical work. Teachers and pupils together have started to believe that handling things at the bench is the main source of understanding, that science lessons are a direct study of nature. My case in this chapter is that the principal object of study should be not nature itself but *sets of ideas*, as represented in the written or spoken words of *people*. Telling about these ideas, and puzzling over them, should be the core of lessons. Apart from improving the quality of learning, I believe this would immediately reinstate the human dimension, and overcome the criticism that science seems dehumanised. It would of course retain the importance of practical work, but place it in a very different light.

Practical work revisited

It has often seemed that the ideal science lesson is one in which pupils are actively engaged in bench work for a lot of their time. We expect to see them busily wiring a circuit with different numbers of bulbs, washing inks across absorbent paper, timing the fall of little parachutes, or soaking wrinkled raisins to see them swell. As teachers we have taken a pride in organising such events, because the pupils handle real materials and we believe that they 'learn by doing' rather than just by being told. We have seen ourselves as 'managers of learning' rather than as didactic dispensers of information. It seems quite odd therefore to question the system, particularly as I do not wish to imply that hands-on experience is not important. Nevertheless, there is a problem.

Practical work seems to offer many opportunities for interpretive activity, as we can say: 'What is going on here? What do you think is happening? Write down what happened'. Unfortunately, that kind of invitation places the pupil not in the reasonable role of interpreting what someone is trying to say, but in the *more difficult* role of interpreting nature. It is a tall order, when thoughtful minds have struggled for decades over the same phenomena! No wonder the experience sometimes fails to boost the self-esteem of the learners, and their confidence in the value of their own ideas!

The solution is to stop thinking of science lessons as the study of nature. Science itself may be a study of nature, but science lessons should be the study of what people have said and thought about nature. The main object of interpretive activity should be not the circuit itself, but *what someone has said about the circuit*, not the events in the test tube alone but *someone's way of talking about them*, not the raisin, but *a written account* of the de-wrinkling, with its words about 'concentrations', 'membranes' and 'permeability', and behind the words an *author*, clearly envisaged as a *human being*. This person, who told the 'story' we are considering: what was he or she trying to say? Science lessons should be the study of systems of meaning which human beings have built up. Practical work is necessary in order to get a feel for those systems, and to give an understanding of what the evidence is which supports the scientific view, but it should not be thought of as the source that ideas come from.

'Word work' for the extraction of ideas

Let me try to represent this recommendation diagramatically, with two kinds of activity – Task A and Task B. If the main object of study is *someone's words*, then the lesson will be planned around those words and not around the circuit board or the test tube. Equipment will be needed, but it will not dominate the time available for study, and there will be time for a proper interplay of tangible experience on the one hand, and interpretive talk and writing on the other. We will have something like the arrangement on the facing page.

Within such a pattern the total time devoted to Word Work (within and between lessons) should exceed that spent on Bench Work. Well-chosen

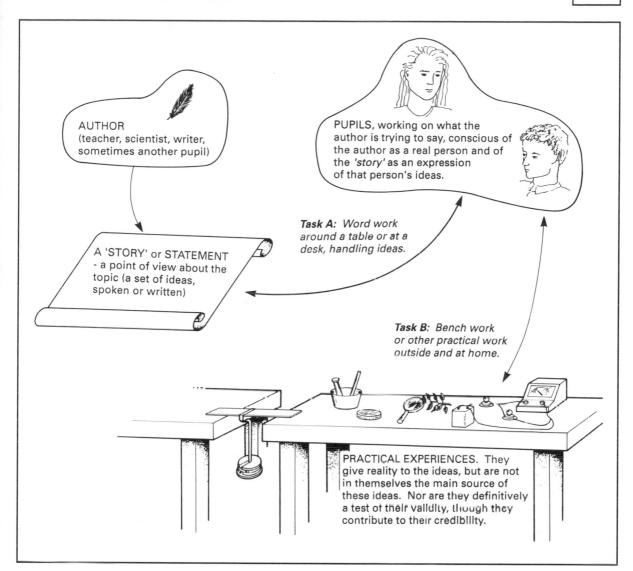

AUTHOR
(teacher, scientist, writer,
sometimes another pupil)

PUPILS, working on what the
author is trying to say, conscious of
the author as a real person and of
the 'story' as an expression
of that person's ideas.

A 'STORY' or STATEMENT
- a point of view about the
topic (a set of ideas,
spoken or written)

*Task A: Word work
around a table or at a
desk, handling ideas.*

*Task B: Bench work
or other practical work
outside and at home.*

PRACTICAL EXPERIENCES. They
give reality to the ideas, but are not
in themselves the main source of
these ideas. Nor are they definitively
a test of their validity, though they
contribute to their credibility.

resource materials appropriate for it are required, and lots of good ideas for organising the work with them. In the past, most of the creativity of science teachers was channelled into organising Task B. The need now is for a corresponding inventiveness in relation to Task A.

Science lessons as appreciation of ideas

It is important that what I have called a '**Story**' or **Statement** in the diagram above is not seen as an account of fact, but as an expression of thought by some *person* who can be identified or at least envisaged. It offers a point of view, a kind of explanation, a way of talking about the topic. It forms the principal material of the lesson. It does not have to be written, though having something on paper can make it easier to argue about. To cater for a wide range of abilities, it will need to take many different forms on different occasions, e.g.:

● something the teacher says, briefly, or writes on the board

- a snippet from a text book
- a newspaper cutting
- two slightly different explanations written by pupils in last year's class
- a snatch of videotape
- a food package label

Sometimes the words of actual scientists may be used – the kind that I have quoted in this book. The art of selecting suitable items is one of considerable subtlety, as they must be capable of leading in to the key talk-system of the topic, and also of engaging the pupils. Usually they must be short, so that there is opportunity to go over the material several times, to comment, interpret, query, and go back to it, as well as to experience the relevant phenomena practically.

The type of science lesson I am describing bears some resemblance to a literature lesson in which the object of appreciation – be it a poem or a prose paragraph – is presented quite quickly, leaving time and scope for reflection, for talk, and for each participant to move towards a considered restatement of their own. Certainly an academic proposition in science, such as $P_1V_1 = P_2V_2$ requires at least as much time and effort to make sense of it, as might be given to a literary one like 'All the world's a stage'. What did the writer mean, and how do we re-create that meaning for ourselves? We could call this 'appreciation of scientific ideas' or even 'meaning extraction'.

Actually there are many classes in which it would not be the best strategy to start with anything like such an academic message as P_1V_1 and all that, but the topic of Boyle's Law has been so long established in science syllabuses that I will stay with it for the moment in a form suitable for an academic group, and use it to illustrate how practical experiences can be short and purposeful, leaving more time for the meaning-extraction activities. Here then are some components for a couple of lessons on the squashability of gases:

(i) A very short **experience** of 'the spring of the air', for everyone individually, squeezing a sealed syringe full of air or another gas.

(ii) A passage such as **Statement 1**, to be read and puzzled over in pairs and trios, leading to some agreed re-statement of what they think the writer was trying to say.

(iii) A short **presentation by the teacher**, with demonstration apparatus, but not using large sections of lesson time to collect experimental results.

(iv) **Practical desk-work** – plotting a graph using second hand data (included in Statement 1), and then a re-statement of what the graph says – made by pupils, with support as necessary.

(v) For an extension, or homework with a high ability group, one could add a further passage such as that in **Statement 2**, in which we can hear Boyle himself speculating about how to account for the spring of the air.[1]

The teacher must be confident of winning the involvement of the pupils in both kinds of task, and there are situations in which it would be easy to take the pessimistic view that only active benchwork will hold the attention of those pupils whose minds seem not so readily drawn to collective thought. That is not an adequate justification for practical work, and anyway such an estimate of pupils' abilities is too pessimistic; it indicates the need for a different task and a changed social relationship, not for abandoning the strategy. In this case I draw some confidence myself from the human interest of Boyle's identification of what he so interestingly called 'the spring of the air'.

For English-speaking pupils, a passage for Statement 1 would more usually be in English, and when I use the word 'interpret' I am not thinking primarily of that special sub-section of interpretive activity which we associate with foreign languages. However, in this case a school book from France does give an added human dimension. What are they saying about this in Paris? Why do they say that? . . . and so on. The technical meaning of the passage hardly differs at all from that in a British book, but its historical and social significance to the French author was different, and there is an opening here for some discussion of the nature of scientific ideas. Data in a foreign language may seem daunting for pupils (and teachers) at first,

STATEMENT 1 L'étude quantitative de la compressibilité des gaz

This is what it says in a French school book, in the section about compressing gases. What are the main points that the writer of the book is trying to make?

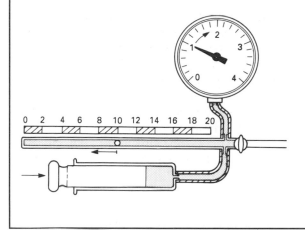

Pour une masse donnée, à température constante, le produit $P \times V$, de la pression et du volume d'un gaz, est constant. C'est la loi de Boyle–Marriotte (*).

* Boyle (1627–91): physicien et chimiste irlandais. Découvrit la loi qui porte son nom en 1661–62, sans l'énoncer clairement.

* Marriotte (1620–84): physicien français. Verifia et précisa la loi de Boyle en 1676, il en donna l'énoncé correct.

Pression (en bar)	0.5	1.0	1.5	1.75	2.0
Volume (en cm³)	20	10	6.7	5.7	5.0

STATEMENT 2 *Boyle's speculations about the reasons for the spring of the air*

Robert Boyle published his most famous account of the air in 1660, and called it *New Experiments Physico-Mechanical, Touching the Spring of the Air and its Effects; Made, for the most Part, in a New Pneumatical Engine*. Some years later he wrote more speculatively about what might account for its springiness:

Of the structure of the elastical particles of the air, divers conceptions may be framed, according to the several contrivances men may devise to answer the phaenomena: for one may think them to be like the springs of watches, coiled up, and still endeavouring to fly abroad. One may also fancy a portion of air to be like a lock or parcel of curled hairs of wool; which being compressed . . . may have a continual endeavour to stretch themselves out, and thrust away the neighbouring particles . . .

I remember too, that I have, among other comparisons of this kind, represented the springy particles of the air like the very thin shavings of wood, that carpenters and joiners are wont to take off with their planers. . . . And perhaps you may the rather prefer this comparison, because . . . these shavings are producible out of bodies, that did not appear, nor were suspected, to be elastical in their bulk, as beams and blocks, almost any of which may afford springy shavings . . . which may perhaps illustrate what I tried, that divers solid . . . bodies, not suspected of elasticity, being put into corrosive menstruums, . . . there will, upon the . . . reaction that passes between them in the dissolution, . . . emerge a pretty quantity of permanently elastical air.

But possibly you will think, that these are but extravagant conjectures; and therefore . . . I shall . . . willingly grant, that one may fancy several other shapes . . . for these springy corpuscles, about whose structure I shall not now particularly discourse. . . . Only I shall here intimate, that though the elastical air seem to continue such, rather upon the score of its structure, than any external agitation; yet heat, that is a kind of motion, may make the agitated particles strive to recede further and further . . . and to beat off those, that would hinder the freedom of their gyrations, and so very much add to the endeavour of such air to expand itself.

And I will allow you to suspect, that there may be sometimes mingled with the particles, that are springy, . . . some others, that owe their elasticity, not so much to their structure, as their motion, which variously brandishing them and whirling them about, may make them beat off the neighbouring particles, and thereby promote an expansive endeavour in the air, whereof they are parts.

> **How many distinctly different ideas does Boyle try out? What impression do you get about which if any of them he prefers, and what is your evidence?**

more so than later experience justifies. Nevertheless, the teacher must judge the match of such a task to the age, experience and confidence of the pupils, and decide whether the task can be 'sold' to them as a worthwhile one, and how much support they may need in order to gain a feeling of success from it.

Statement 2 contains some very difficult language, but I think it is not appropriate to simplify it and replace it by teachers' words on paper. The result would too easily seem like something to be learned rather than something to be puzzled over. I would feel the same if the data page were part of a modern technical manual on car engine compression ratios. The place for simplification is in the *speech* of both pupils and teachers, where difficult expressions can be taken alongside their more everyday equivalents.[2]

Many lessons on Boyle's Law have no doubt been intended to have a structure of the kind I have described, dwelling on the appreciation of the idea. I think, however, that unless interpretation of meaning of the written word is advertised and proclaimed as the main purpose of the lesson, too much of the available time can be used in collecting figures from experimental equipment. The impact of the lesson then is not of engaging the learners' minds with great scientific thoughts, but just of passing on authoritative knowledge.

Returning to the comparison of a science lesson and a literature lesson, probably there should be no fundamental difference, because in each case some person's meaning has to be sorted out and re-created in the minds of the learners. In a science lesson it is an advantage that we have access to tangible experience, but this cannot replace the interpretive work that must be done. Bench work should be primarily an aid to extracting the meaning from the words, and checking one's own interpretation of them. Pupils may seem to be checking Boyle's Law, but what they should be checking is their own idea of what Boyle meant, and how he came to that view.

Types of interpretive activity

In British schools, over-reliance on bench work may have passed its peak in the 1970s, when published schemes were characterised by long sequences of practical worksheet after practical worksheet. Moves to diversify learning activities are found in the more recent curriculum projects, and there is much talk of 'flexible learning and a *range* of teaching and learning strategies'. One guide for writers of new material for publication gives a list, of which the following is an abbreviated version.

Ways of Learning: A checklist of (overlapping) approaches[3]

- by watching and listening
- by doing bench or field work, to a plan which someone else made for you
- by practical investigations which *you* plan, or help to plan

- by interpreting and evaluating data from charts, tables, graphs, etc.
- by tackling a technological problem, where you *try to design a solution*
- by *discussing ideas in a small group*

- by *writing – putting ideas together for an audience other than the teacher*
- by close reflective reading

- by teaching: *presenting a short talk or a poster to explain ideas to other students*
- by *devising maps, diagrams and charts* to express and communicate ideas
- by *taking part in role-plays*, simulations, and games

- by manipulating ideas and information with a computer
- by searching through audio-tapes, slides and video resource materials
- by careful analysis of 'case-studies' of events outside school

---

In adult education or other sectors of the secondary school, such a list would not look at all strange, but for science teachers these activities are not so obviously right and necessary. 'Discussing ideas in small groups' surely lends itself to waffle, and 'writing for an audience other than the teacher' sounds a bit peripheral, and not what pupils expect to do in science. As for drama and role play, that might be nice for a change, but is it really learning science? And if someone suggests that pupils should prepare speeches for a debate, it definitely seems like an extra rather than a crucial part of the learning. Debates are associated with opinions rather than with the consolidation of factual knowledge – more suitable for current affairs than for a science lesson.

The non-bench activities therefore have a somewhat uncertain status, not quite accepted by pupils or teachers as part of the real learning of science, and for that reason they may not be exploited to the full. Sometimes they are recommended on the common sense view that variety is a good thing, and the best way to avoid the boredom of repetitive routines. Although we do need variety, it would be a pity if these activities were seen only in that way. Part of my purpose in this book has been to express a rationale within which they can be seen to be more central to the learning. If pupils and their parents, as well as teachers, understand the need for interpretive effort, then the writing or the role-play will be used more positively for that purpose. To design a carefully thought-out flow-chart on a poster, or to get ready to speak about it to the class, or to work out on paper how to explain to a younger child what (say) 'pasteurisation' is – these are exactly the tasks which make an appropriately high level of demand on the pupils, and require interpretive effort of them. With care, they also enable teachers to provide a supportive environment in which to encourage that effort. Diversified activities are not luxuries and extras, but necessary to the process of getting pupils to grapple with the ideas of science. Without them, I suggest that the bench work will continue to alienate as many pupils as it excites, and to leave others quite untouched by these ideas.

There is, however, the question of professional skills. A science teacher who can get an oscilloscope to work does not necessarily feel confident in organising a role-play, or in motivating pupils to set out their written reports for a non-scientific audience. Such skills were formerly outside the province of the science teacher, and although they are now being learned, it is not in any systematic way. They are self-taught by enthusiasts and passed on slowly to others.[4] There are many helpful techniques which will either have to be assimilated to the repertoire of science teachers' skills, or else we shall need more differentiation of teachers' roles, with some members of the team specialising more in preparing pupils to work over ideas while others provide the backup of well-organised practical experience.

Kinds of resource material

In Britain, the most extensive collection of resources to stimulate alternative activities is found in the SATIS units – *Science and Technology in Society*.[5] They offer a great diversity of activity and place in the hands of pupils data which are both more problematic than commonly found in a science textbook, and of much greater human interest. Using them generally involves much more talking, discussing and interpreting, relative to the standard bench work. Does such material automatically switch teachers and learners into a different style of language use, or does the rationale have to be made explicit? Many SATIS activities can be justified on several different grounds, not the least of which is that they are fun, but often the gains might be greater if parents and pupils were quite clear that (say) a technological problem is being set in order for the pupils to clarify their understanding of the relevant scientific concepts in their own words. A few examples of activities are listed on the following page.

Most of these units provide material which requires the readers to get at the writer's intention, and to re-express it for themselves. They are a direct stimulus to word work as I have described it, and they make it legitimate for the learner to have a point of view based on a clear understanding of relevant science, in a way which textbooks and instruction sheets do not. This is one of the reasons

Title of SATIS unit	Activities
The limestone enquiry	Analysing technical data, identifying by discussion the relevant facts and issues for consideration at a Planning Enquiry about a quarry extension, discussion of briefing papers for groups making representations at the enquiry, presenting ideas in a role-play of it.
X-rays and patients	Analysing technical documents; selecting and presenting information in a form suitable for patients in a waiting room.
The label at the back	A survey at home of fabrics and their uses; collating the information and presenting a summary, with explanation.
The re-trial of Galileo	Studying role-description cards, identifying ideas important to original participants; discussing each role, then playing them in a dramatised re-enactment of the trial.

why a technological problem is sometimes a better starting point for learning some science than is direct study of the science itself. Technological problems are not closed-ended, and it is usually clear that more than one solution is acceptable, so it is easier for a learner to put forward an idea which draws on scientific knowledge, without fear of looking foolish. It is also easier for the teacher to be open to varied suggestions, whereas when discussion of a scientific problem directly is attempted it is hard for a teacher to avoid the trap of searching the class for the 'expected' answer, and greeting others with such faint praise that genuine discussion dies out.

SATIS-type activities will not automatically lead into the clarification of the full vocabulary and network of concepts in the related scientific topics, unless pupils and teacher approach them with that intention in mind. They are, however, a way of engaging the minds of the learners, placing them in positions of initiative in relation to ideas, and giving them a different concept of the part played by their own use of language in their learning.

Maintaining the learner's freedom

Freedom of interpretation is a key feature of good resource materials. There should be enough doubt in them to set the pupil's mind moving, and keep it moving, and also it should be legitimate for the

doubt to lead to more than one acceptable conclusion, so that anyone may make reasoned estimates of the meaning without fear of being totally wrong. Under those circumstances language will naturally be used to explore what is meant, what was intended, and what we now understand. Teaching and learning will involve a degree of negotiation of the meaning: 'This is what I think is meant; how do you and other people understand it?' Some activities designed to support inexperienced readers work by artificially increasing the amount of uncertainty about what is being said.[6] In this connection, the power of narrative material about science seems to have been neglected. We know that a story can hold average readers much more easily than other kinds of writing, and Bruner[7] points out that narrative prose exerts its effect by recruiting the reader's imagination and triggering presupposition about what may be coming next, or what underlies what has already been said. The reader's mind is working on what is *not* present on the page, as well as what is there. The lack of explicit spelling out of every aspect is the feature which makes it possible for the reader to enter into and engage with the story. It offers freedom to do that, whereas explicitness would reduce the freedom, and hence the degree of involvement with the text. Perhaps one reason why a factual account of a scientific topic in a textbook often fails to hold attention is that it does not leave enough doubt, or lead the reader to fill it out from his or her own thought. There are not enough cues to uncertain possibilities to keep the average reader thinking ahead. Of course scientific books make a virtue of spelling things out, and leaving no doubt. Here is one of several places where features appropriate to science itself are not so appropriate for education.

For the future we may need two types of reading material – one to encourage the exploration of scientific ideas, the other to form a reliable quick guide to their structure. The traditional textbook is the latter only. There is also a case for making a clear division between two different kinds of lesson – one called 'Exploring scientific ideas' and the other 'Learning the systematics of science'. In the first of these, the freedom of the learner could be preserved absolutely, with a rule that there are no assumptions about 'right answers'; we are just exploring what people have thought and said about scientific matters. The teacher's role could be unambiguously one of encouraging and supporting speech and writing by the pupils, and the resources for these lessons would be of the types already discussed. In the second kind of lesson it would then be more legitimate to present the currently accepted structures of thought through clear exposition, without encroaching on the freedom of the learner to think. A relatively old-fashioned style of textbook, as a grammar of the subject, would also have its rightful place in that second kind of lesson, so avoiding the confusions of recent years when so-called 'textbooks' have attempted to do too many things at once (see Chapter 10).

Support for the interpretive writer

What happens to pupils' writing is of crucial importance if the habit of using language interpretively is to be established. The individual learner's idea of what writing is for can be extensively shaped by the attitudes of the teacher, and what the teacher explicitly or implicitly encourages. Teachers therefore need to be aware of the power of their taken-for-granted routines. For pupils to make full use of writing for the purpose of

sorting out meaning probably requires the system of intermittent dialogue between teacher and pupil about what they write, a system which has been fully described elsewhere.[8]

Factors which matter include:

1 What the teacher does with pupils' writing when it has been completed.
2 The amount of time spent beforehand on discussing the purpose of the writing, its possible form and content, expectations in terms of style, and reasons for these.
3 The writer's sense of audience while attempting to set down ideas.
4 The extent to which the teacher allows and encourages a variety of styles.

All these are all deeply affected by the teacher's beliefs about what the writing is for. An extended account of these beliefs has recently been published by Douglas Barnes,[8] and I shall outline the main features of old and new traditions over writing in science lessons in the next chapter (pages 89–90).

Social and emotional climate

None of what I have described in this chapter can occur unless appropriate social relationships are established between teacher and pupils and amongst the pupils themselves. Much of this book has been about the cognitive functions of language, and I had better acknowledge therefore that in the classroom it is the emotional functions which have priority. What, for example is happening in the following exchanges?

TEACHER: Gather round here please . . . One at a time now . . . Listen to Vijay . . . I think you can make a good job of the graph, can't you?

PUPILS: Do we have to do it now? . . . I'm no good at graphs . . . [and later] Hey, Miss, it really works!

It would be silly to seek the importance of what is said here just in terms of the instruction or information that seems to pass. Questions of feeling, of a learner's self-concept, and of organisation and social control, are threaded through the words; they remind us that language has many functions in addition to the interpretation of ideas.[9] At the simplest level, there is often a direct clash in the classroom between using language to encourage thought, and using it for social control. For example, when teachers are helping pupils to elaborate their first thoughts, and to gain confidence in reasoning out an idea, they use long attentive pauses,[10] yet a common and successful technique for the management of large groups involves a kind of dominance strategy with very short pauses in the teacher's delivery!

To adopt an interpretive view of language requires a certain kind of social relationship between teacher and taught which we could describe as one of enhanced respect for the learner and the learner's ideas, so the only possible strategy is to accompany him or her on a journey in thought. As a teacher one needs to have rather less confidence in the obviousness and rightness of one's own way, or the textbook way of explaining the phenomenon under discussion. And of course, the first task in teaching is not to arrange the subject matter, but to gathering the minds of the learners, to a point where one can say:

Well, Vijay, and Alan, and Mary, what do you think these people had in mind when they put it that way?

Notes

1 Boyle's speculations: See Marie Boas Hall (1965) *Robert Boyle on Natural Philosophy – an essay with selections from his writings*, Indiana University Press, Bloomington.

2 Is simplification of language desirable in science education? My view is that 'the language problem' of the science classroom is not adequately solved by adjusting 'readability levels' downwards, or by trying to avoid technical terms. It is more to do with an absence of encouragement for flexibility of expression, for putting the same idea in more than one way. Ideally this flexibility should be shown first in speech, and then not discouraged in writing. A word like 'elastic' means more when 'squashable', 'stretchable', 'resilient' and 'compressible' are used along-

side it, rather than as a replacement for it, and of course they show that there is something about the material which we are trying to interpret, not just to label. Teachers can show the value of this flexibility firstly by practising for themselves the habit of using both technical and less technical phrasing, and then by accepting and understanding the learner's struggles in the same direction.

Some degree of difficulty in the material to be read is actually a help in providing incentive for the learners to 'decode' it and make a restatement in their own words. To translate everything into simpler language also carries a risk of being condescending. Pupils are entitled to expect that they will be taught how to cope with technical, and even abstruse, language, and we should get them into the habit of doing so. Where pupils are very unconfident readers, the best strategy seems to me not to re-write ideas for them, but to select more suitable written materials from real life, which are just a little above their present level of coping. If the label on the new shoe says '100% synthetic materials' or even 'polybutadiene' that is something to be grappled with, not avoided.

3 Ways of learning: Andrew Hunt (1991), personal communication. The list on which I have drawn was prepared for writers of learning episodes within the publication programme of the Nuffield Modular Science Project.

4 Professional skills for the management of interpretive activities: A programme of professional development in this field would involve workshops on the management of writing, reading, role-play, etc. The manner of focusing thought and feeling on the occasions where these activities are to work well is not the same as getting the class ready for practical work at the bench. Professional development for this work would also have to provide background in the history of ideas, which many science teachers have not got from their own higher education.

5 SATIS units are published by the Association for Science Education, Hatfield. (i) John Holman (ed.) (1986) *Science and Technology in Society: Teaching units and Teacher's Guide*, ASE, Hatfield; (ii) Andrew Hunt (ed.) (1990) *SATIS 16–19*, from the same source.

6 Structured reading activities: increasing uncertainty in order to engage the reader's active search for meaning. Two of the best-known activities which exaggerate the uncertainty to a level which will give readers' minds a more direct task to work on are:

(i) Sequencing a scrambled text and arguing the reasons for that sequence, and

(ii) reconstructing missing portions – not just odd words, but larger sections as when (say) the edge of the paper has been destroyed or 'lost'

These and other such activities have become more widely known since the work of the Reading for Learning Project and they are called DARTs ('directed activities related to text'). See F. Davies and T. Greene (1979) *Reading for Learning in Science*, University of Nottingham School of Education. Both the quoted methods offer the interest of a detective hunt, and both can be powerful because they require the reader *to build up a general idea of what is being said*, and from this to predict the missing parts, or argue what the order of presentation must have been. Such devices must be used sensitively, and the reconstruction game should not be confused with the very different process of asking pupils to fill in missing words here and there, which frequently stimulates hardly any general interpretive effort. Also because the modified passages are artificially contrived, they could quickly pall in over-use. A better long-term support to active engagement with reading would be to break the monopoly now held by informative non-fiction, and offer more science books and booklets which have a strong narrative thread, as well as more reading materials of the SATIS type which come from sources other than books.

7 Narrative prose and its effect on the reader's free-dom of interpretation: See Jerome Bruner (1986) *Actual Minds, Possible Worlds*, Harvard University Press, e.g. p. 25, and also Chapter 9, 'The language of education'.

8 Support for the interpretive writer, dialogue marking, etc.: See Peter Benton (1981) 'Writing – how it is received' and Owen Watkins (1981) 'Writing – how it is set', both in C. R. Sutton (ed.) *Communicating in the Classroom*, Hodder and Stoughton, 10th impression, 1991.

Teachers' beliefs about the purposes of writing: See Yanina Sheeran, Douglas Barnes (1991) *School Writing*, Open University Press, especially Chapter 2, 'Scientific language'.

9 The many functions of language. See David Crystal in *The Cambridge Encyclopaedia of Language* (Cambridge University Press, 1987). He discusses a range of functions for language, amongst which are the following, in my order, not his: recording the facts; as an instrument of thought; as an expression of identity; for control of reality; for social interaction; emotional expression; phonetic pleasure.

Scientific language is often seen as mainly for recording facts, whereas I have been giving more prominence to its use as an instrument of thought. Its role in developing a sense of social identity for members of the scientific community, and for pupils in a classroom, deserves much more attention.

10 Language for social control: For an account of the role of attentive pausing, see Mary Budd Rowe (1973) 'Science silence and sanctions' in *Teaching Science as Continuous Enquiry*, McGraw-Hill.

CHAPTER 10

Questions of style

In addition to the large amount of time given to practical work, there are many other traditions of working in school science which combine to diminish the interpretive use of language, and the purpose of this chapter is to examine them as traditions, rather than necessities. What is, or was, their purpose? Are they essential to an education in science, or merely fashions which could be changed without loss? I think of all of them as working styles, using 'style' in a very broad sense to include not only the overall style of a lesson as discussed in Chapter 9, but also:

- **the style of the rooms in which we work**
- **styles of writing by pupils**
- **styles of writing for pupils**

Styles of rooms

Secondary school science has had its own rooms and special equipment for over a century, and if learners are to connect the ideas of science properly with tangible experience, it is essential that there should be adequate space and material for safe practical work. School managers have a responsibility to provide an environment to make it possible. On the other hand, for learning to be based on an active interpretive use of language, the form of the facilities is due for a substantial re-think.

Many laboratories in secondary schools do not now look like the one illustrated on page 84, but nevertheless they are its direct descendants.

School rooms often express the assumptions which their designers made about how learning will occur,[1] and once they are established, the rooms themselves shape the activities of those who inhabit them, and create a culture in which people think there is no other way to work. So what was this room in the picture for? What assumptions about learning can we detect? In particular, what expectations did it embody about the role of language in learning?

It is certainly not intended for a lecture by the teacher, transmitting verbal information. The room says to us, and to the public at large, that chemistry is a practical subject: the handling of chemicals is very important. Speaking of any kind has perhaps a lower priority, but we should remember that there was often a section, or another room next door, where the teacher could hold forth with words, and also demonstrate many practical things. The room contains no specific provision for any of the learners to make a public statement to the rest, either after handling the chemicals ('This is what I think was happening') or beforehand ('My first thoughts are that the substance is probably . . . and so I expect that it will . . . because . . .'). Teachers may have given over the demonstration bench from time to time to members of the class for that kind of thought-developing statement, but it is not a standard expectation built into the planning of the facilities. The facilities do not help to maintain any belief in its importance. When pupils work in such a room, their active statement of ideas in speech is easily

Chemistry laboratory added to the Wyggeston Boys' School, High Cross Street, Leicester, in 1895, as seen through the eyes of the art master, Mr G. S. Catlow. (From the original water colour, now in the archives of the Wyggeston and Queen Elizabeth Sixth Form College, Leicester.)

left to chance rather than being a specifically planned event.

Our modern laboratories are scarcely any better in that respect. Current ideas of learning do suggest that pupils should formulate a clear statement of their existing ideas at several stages, and one way is for them to talk in small groups, prepare a poster, and then try to explain it to the rest of the class. Where are the areas, in a modern laboratory, for that kind of activity, for putting up the poster, or seating the other pupils in comfortable positions, so that their minds can engage with what is being said? The ideal modern room would cater for discussion, for display of pupils' work, and perhaps also for clearing the floor for other activities such as role-play, mentioned in Chapter 9. In all probability this could be achieved at no extra cost and within the space currently available, but the traditional laboratory layout continues to

influence what is built, and how people use it. Those who teach in newer buildings may have movable tables which can be pushed back and rearranged, but the extent to which that is actually done is limited not only by the furniture itself, but by the dominance of the idea that hands-on practical is the major activity.

Modern benches retain the spirit of the older forms partly because it is held that pupils must have easy access to power and water supply, which are often still fed to the middle of the room, if not inside a fixed bench, then in bollards, or in overhead piping. Good work in science certainly does require access to such services, but does it really need two or three sinks on every bench, which are there all day and every day? What about the influence of those sinks at times when the activity is supposed to be 'listening to the teacher' or 'watching a demonstration' or 'taking part in a discussion', or 'quiet writing'? How often is the swan-necked tap actually used for the purposes for which it was designed? To arrange any of the activities mentioned in Chapter 9 in the average school science laboratory, one has to work against the facilities rather than being helped by them. Discussion will often fail if people cannot sit facing each other, and more so if a portion of the teacher's effort is absorbed in regaining the attention of those who face the window. Even the call to 'Gather round the front now please' will not automatically ease communication. With pupils unsurely seated or standing, the atmosphere of the moment has to be created and maintained by constant effort of the teacher. The facilities of most rooms do not help to maintain it, and it is hardly surprising that some modern teenagers should be restless in such a situation. All this is tolerated because of a belief that the bench work is what matters most.

Rooms of the traditional kind support a limited range of activity because they were not designed for the educational goals we now hope to attain in universal secondary education, i.e. helping the learners to understand the world outside school through a grasp of scientific concepts. In physics they were for learning some of the procedures which physicists then used, and in chemistry you could learn to do what chemists did. Working in these rooms served as an induction into some of the procedures of the discipline. We can see this most strongly if we consider the notebooks on the benches. What were the learners writing? For part

of the time in chemistry they would be writing reports about the qualitative analysis of an unknown substance or a mixture – i.e. identifying its constituents without measuring how much of each was present. One of the systems that the novice analysts were taught, as a way of keeping a record, involved three columns headed Test, Observation and Inference. It is not a system which guides you in the whole cycle of thought needed for a successful analysis, because it does not require you to articulate reasons why any particular test should be chosen, and there is no hint of thoughts in advance, or of what you expect might happen. It does however make sense in the context of professional apprenticeship because it builds up a record which can form an adequate defence of the overall conclusion made at the end: 'This powder contains a carbonate, and the main metal present is lead', or whatever. An important part of being a scientist is the habit and skill of making that kind of record. It is important however to distinguish between 'learning to keep a scientific record' and the very different process of 'learning to understand scientific ideas'.

Two other kinds of record kept in those early school chemistry laboratories were of gravimetric analysis – getting the composition of some material by weight, and volumetric analysis, a more convenient though indirect route to similar conclusions. In both cases there was great stress on the manner of laying out the results – a good training in presenting defensible conclusions. Physics notebooks of the same period were often works of great

Weight of bottle = 14·321 grams
Weight of bottle full of water = 64·461 grams
Weight of bottle full of Methylated Spirits = 55·09 grams
∴ Weight of 50 ccs. of water = 50·140 grs
∴ Weight of 50 ccs of Methylated Spirits = 40·669 grms
∴ Relative Density of Methylated Spirits = 1·23 grams

News item included in the first edition of 'Nature', November 1869

The Editors applaud the work of Dr. Frederick Temple, and describe the laboratories he founded at Rugby school. The suite of rooms they mention set a trend in expectations of what science teaching in British schools could be like.

By offering Dr. Temple the Bishopric of Exeter, Mr Gladstone has removed from his post the most eminent schoolmaster in England. Dr. Temple has done much for the education . . . we may note here what he has done for education in Science.

He may fairly claim to be the first head-master who has recognised its importance, and effectively introduced it into his school. And its introduction at Rugby is of special importance, because it is the acknowledged leader in educational progress, and because so many head-masters have been trained there. Now Harrow and Eton, and several other schools are doing something, though none yet with quite the same liberality as Rugby: but it will be instructive to look back ten years, and thus to estimate the advance. Rugby was then the only public school where science was taught at all. But even there it was under great disadvantages. No school was assigned to it; it was an extra, and heavily weighed by extra payment. There was no laboratory, scarcely any apparatus, and scarcely any funds for promoting it. About forty to fifty boys attended lectures on it, but there was no possibility of making those lectures consecutive, and of dealing with advanced pupils. Now there is a suite of rooms devoted to science.

A large and excellent laboratory, where thirty boys are working at the same time at practical chemistry with the assistance of a laboratory superintendent, opens into a smaller private laboratory which is for the use of the master and a few advanced students. This again opens into a chemical lecture room, in which from forty to fifty can conveniently sit. The seats are raised, and the lecture table fitted with all that is required. Adjoining is the physical science lecture room, in which sixty can sit, and of which a part is assigned to work tables. And out of this the master's private room is reached, in which apparatus is kept, and experiments and work prepared. . . .

And the result of the teaching has been satisfactory. It has not damaged classics. It has been the means of educating many boys, and has been a visible gain to the great majority; and it has steadily contributed to the lists of honours gained at the University.

If Dr Temple had done nothing else, his name would deserve honour at our hand for having brought about this change. Let us hope that his successor will be equally liberal to science, and maintain its efficiency.

---

craftsmanship, with double-page spreads showing, for example, how 'To find the specific gravity of methylated spirit using a relative density bottle'. For those going into laboratories where the craft of exact measurement would be required, the experience of making such a report at least offered a clear example to follow, and the techniques themselves were all professionally relevant at some stage.

In summary we can say of the picture on page 84 that both the school room itself and its procedures were modelled on the corresponding laboratory of the working scientist. The tradition of setting up school science in that way continued for most of the twentieth century, with various modernisations of equipment and techniques. It seemed the 'obvious' thing to do, for surely an important reason for teaching science in school is to recruit a future generation of scientists? Certainly the leaders of British science in the later Victorian decades were glad to applaud the provision of such facilities, as we can see in the extract above from the first edition of the journal *Nature*.

To have youngsters in schools doing something like what scientists do, in rooms something like where scientists work, was bound to be gratifying to the professionals, but is it a good way to give more people an understanding of science? Recruitment of future scientists remains one of the objectives of school science, but now this is within a wider set of aims to do with the education of the citizenry at large, and so the correctness of the approach can no longer be taken for granted. It cannot be assumed that a school experience which simply models the craft skills of professional scientists will captivate all youngsters, or even all those whom we might hope to recruit to science.

Styles of writing: Reporting what you did

Just as rooms in secondary schools were set up for the learners to do what scientists did, so the writing asked of them gave practice in certain limited kinds which feature in the work of a scientist – **keeping a careful record**, and **making a report**. Where the purpose was definitely professional training this policy could perhaps be justified, but it will be clear from examples given in this book that real scientists write in a variety of styles. Why then has there been such a preference for one limited area of writing, and how do we account for the persistent belief that the stylistic features it incorporates are somehow better or more scientific than others, and that science teachers have a duty to instil them? I look for the reasons in a combination of factors:

- in what science teachers learned from their own mentors
- in a tacit assumption that training youngsters in how to keep scientific records was a main part of the job
- in the high status therefore accorded to laboratory reports as compared with other possible forms of writing
- in a general preference for objectified styles which has affected all academic writing in the twentieth century, with suppression of personal interpretation

Scientific reports themselves have not always been made in a wholly impersonal style, and it is not fundamental to them, though the attempt to distance the observer from the report has been a recurring feature, for sound reasons. In this century, as numbers of scientists seeking publication has increased, de-personalised prose has become the standard way of signalling that distancing.

Having the scientist's first report of experiments as the dominant model of how to write produced an imbalance in pupils' writing – imbalance between **reporting** on the one hand, and **explaining** on the other. Almost without realising it we created a regime in which language for reporting unarguable information came to prominence week after week and month after month, at the expense of that for explaining, justifying, and exploring uncertainty.

To understand the effects of this imbalance, I want to consider what the purposes of an initial report by a scientist are, and some purposes it does not have. Notably, a report sent by a scientist to a journal is not for the purpose of explaining ideas to an audience of people unfamiliar with the topic. Its language may look obscure, but the immediate readers for whom it is intended are other workers in the same field, and for them it is clear and highly economical. The paper concentrates on setting out an account of procedures used in some investigation, and the results claimed to have been found. Details of equipment and materials are given in a way which is intended to allow someone else to try to repeat the work if they wish, with – as it were – the challenge to find anything other than the same results. Sentence constructions with the third person and the passive voice are not strictly necessary, but they make sense in such a report, indicating the way in which someone else could do the work again: 'The flasks were gently shaken for 5 hours on a rotary shaker at one rotation per second.'

Secondly, a journal account is not a complete recapitulation of a full chain of reasoning, from ideas to ways of testing them, to findings. Discussion of the significance of the results is relatively subservient to their presentation, and the introductory parts of the paper contextualise the investigation briefly as following from certain other results reported in such and such other journal. Just how the earlier report led to any new thoughts and how fresh predictions worth testing were formulated is often omitted altogether, as are the detailed reasons for choosing one set of conditions rather than another. Journal editors do not give space for accounts of the **having ideas** part of science, but only for the **testing ideas** part. This incompleteness does not matter very much because scientists have other ways of communicating, in congresses and seminars, where theoretical ideas are explored in a less clinical way. It matters in school, though, and before demanding the imitation of such writing in the classroom on a regular basis, we should have been alert to the possible consequences of letting pupils habitually not tell the whole story of their thought, and habitually not strive to meet an uninitiated audience. How are they to gain confidence in their own ability to sort out ideas? How are they or the teacher to know what they fully comprehend? What image of science do they get from such writing?

Elsewhere[2] I have traced in detail how the journal account exerted its influence on school writing, and what the effect has been on people's image of science. I shall summarise the main points below, but we should note that it has also shaped ideas about what counts as science education. The preference for a set format encouraged the view that the important objective is to give pupils a training in scientific writing. It held back teachers' experimentation with writing as a means for developing understanding. Test–Observation–Inference was only one of the standard formats, and various versions of METHOD–RESULTS–CONCLUSION were more pervasive. Although such a rigid pattern is now much less common, many expectations which accompanied it survive and influence current practice, so I will recapitulate here some key points about it.

1 Early in their secondary school experience pupils picked up what was expected and allowable in their writing for a science teacher.

> There were what Douglas Barnes calls the 'ground rules' – implicit standards which pupils had to infer from the teacher's behaviour, and which established 'the way you talk in school', 'the way you talk in science' and 'the way you write in science'. Some pupils had difficulties in

reading the cues that signal these expectations, but most shaped their language to conform to the implicit norms of this new world. Comments made by teachers on the child's earliest written work were powerful in shaping such conformity.

2 They came to associate writing in science, not with sorting out what you understand, but more with making an acceptable record of practical work.

- You had to say what you did ('Method'), and then to say what happened (or what should have happened) ('Results'). These two parts dominated the effort and imagination of the learners.
- If the teacher specified other headings, such as 'Aim' and 'Conclusion', these often caused difficulty, but there were ways of coping. 'Aim' could generally be reduced to a title, decided directly or indirectly by the teacher; 'Conclusions' could be postponed by taking longer over the middle parts, and then asking the teacher.

The classical writing systems thus elevated doing above thinking, especially above thinking beforehand, and so they gave a misleading impression of science as 'describing what happens'. Teachers themselves regarded the aim or purpose of any laboratory work as the starting point for it, but for pupils, the reason for doing anything was easily read as 'Teacher says', and it was possible to survive without entering into the preliminary reasoning.

Current attempts to develop pupil's confidence in Planning investigations (part of Attainment Target 1 of the National Curriculum) may change this situation. If a system of headings has to be used, then 'first ideas', 'plans and predictions', 'actions' and 'later thoughts' may shift the pupils' perceptions of what is needed and possible, but can we be sure that it will?

3 Many teachers, realising that writing in the third person was not necessary, tried to make the approach more child-centred and personal, by translating the headings into 'What we did', 'What we saw' and 'What we thought'.

> They had some success in bringing out the thought processes of the learners, but often 'I did . . .' still remained more prominent than

'I thought . . .' 'We stirred the mixture in a beaker, and we saw it go solid', prevailed, rather than 'We decided to stir the mixture and not to heat it because . . .'.

4 An influential factor in maintaining this approach to writing, and in sustaining such guidance from teachers as 'Describe what happened' was the Baconian view of science, which is discussed in Chapter 11.

If we understand the history of writing in school science we may be able to escape the dominance of one objective – **practising how to write a scientific report**. It is a reasonable part of science education, but not every day! It has distorted, and in some cases eliminated, other writing, i.e. **writing in order to understand a scientist's ideas**, which should be a constant theme in learning any new topic.

The most obvious way to avoid a confusion of the two objectives is to make the formal report-writing an occasional event, so that it can be done really well, with the teacher explaining both the form and function of a tight defence of evidence. The learners can then get a good understanding of the rules of that game, and know when they have succeeded at that kind of writing. The rest of the time is then free for a full exploitation of other forms which relate the learner's thought more effectively to the topics being studied. On these other occasions there need be no suggestion that there is only one way to write, and 'you have to do it that way or it isn't science'. Reluctance to say 'I think . . . because . . .' could then be a thing of the past.

Other styles of writing: Sorting out what you understand

Strangely, it is not at all obvious how best to guide pupils in these other forms of writing and to make them really effective for processing and re-processing ideas. Rather few people of any age are spontaneously confident at expressing their partly-formed ideas on paper, and parents and pupils have a very uncertain image of the kinds of activity which help you to do so. Also, the teacher's role in relation to such work, which contains more of the listener and less of the assessor, is not widely understood. There is therefore an urgent need to publish collections of such work, sorted by topic and age group, with notes on how the pupils and their teachers prepared for it, what the pupils learned, and how we can be sure of that. For many teachers there is still a suspicion that it will come down to 'creative writing' which does not grapple with concepts, or to 'Design an advertisement for soap', or 'Write a poem about the ozone layer' or some other definitely lightweight lesson. Of course, even those may have a valuable place, but sometimes they turn out to be condescending, and do not help to build up the pupils' own estimates of what they can do. We should not accept too low a level of aspiration, or adopt the pessimistic view of pupils' abilities. The challenge to the teacher is to devise small tasks which will capture the imagination of the learner, and give a target audience for whom it is necessary to clarify ideas. As I have mentioned in the previous chapter, the keys to success appear to be:

- the clarity of **writer's sense of audience**,
- the amount of **preparation** done before the writing begins, thinking it through, talking it over, considering what is needed in this particular situation, and
- **how the teacher responds** to the product.

Science teachers are used to setting written work rather quickly at the end of a long lesson of practical work, and the preparation is easily missed. Then, when the pupils do not cope very well it is easy to blame their 'inability', and not to try such tasks again, when all that was needed was more preparation and confidence building.

At many points in learning, the obvious audience to explain your ideas to is the trusted teacher, as those who have learned by correspondence know, but often it will sharpen the mind to have to write for some other group of people, real or imagined. A 'Let's pretend' audience needs particularly good preparation, and should not be over-used, unless the teacher can create the sense of play which will allow it over and over again. Suppose they are pretending to write for the Leicester Canning Corporation about what metals to consider for the cans for their next thousand kilos of stewed raspberries. Can we truly help them to make the necessary imaginative leap? Such an audience does not have to be addressed directly every time, and it will sometimes be better for the teacher to say: 'Let's prepare the kind of information we would need if we had to report to the company. What are the main points to be made about the various metals? What do we know about their properties? Would they, for example, react with the fruit juice?'

Real audiences can also be found – pupils in a twinned school,[3] parents, even school Governors, but these too should not be over-used! A task of genuine responsibility, like designing safety labels which will be used in the school, can sharpen the quality of the writing, and help the teacher to take the role of coach rather than assessor. Inventive teachers have a great variety of such tasks at many levels of difficulty, and some are very successful in making themselves an accessible audience, so that the writers really *want* to explain:[3]

- Tell *me* what you think the ancient apparatus shown in this diagram was for; how do *you* think it worked? Draw a sequence of diagrams to show your idea of how it worked, stage by stage. What was its designer trying to achieve? [various ages]
- Here are two scripts from last year's class. Was there any mistake in Andrew's answer? What were the best points in Maria's? [age 13]
- Take any two key words from the topic of vibrations and waves, and make an acrostic which will show us something important about what you have learned [age 13]
- Can we really understand refraction using the analogy of a marching column of soldiers crossing from tarmac onto grass? Convince us! [age 15]
- Set out your diagram of a food chain in a form suitable for parents' evening [age 13]
- Make a numbered step by step instruction list [various ages]
- After studying the ancient and modern methods

of iron smelting, write a diary of a charcoal-burner's working day [age 13]
- Read this obituary of a scientist cut from the newspaper. What do you think the writer felt about the dead person, and what is your evidence? What were the main things that the dead person will be remembered for? [age 15]

When pupils are confident of using writing as a means of working over ideas there is also an important role for 'daft' and humorous writing – for some adolescents the crazier the better in order to capitalise on their alertness, and keep them on their toes. Many are quite able to respond in kind to the fun-poking style of writers like Keith Johnson (see p. 92). Most important is the learner's personal involvement with the task, and hence the sense of its being his or her own product.

Another kind of writing: Completing the set worksheet

For reasons which are only partly connected with a change in the balance of objectives, writing in science lessons in British schools did change quite dramatically after the mid 1970s, with a decrease in the amount of extended writing of any kind. As comprehensive schools developed, science teachers encountered teenagers of the full range of ability and achievement, including some for whom extended writing was only 'a way that teachers keep us quiet', an essentially unpleasant, difficult experience and a source of anxiety. These pupils certainly would not settle easily to the traditional writing, and the first reaction was to break up the class and set small group work supervised by worksheets needing only short answers to structured questions. It seemed a feasible way of organising a mixed-ability class, but many of the first generation of such worksheets relied heavily on recipe-type instructions, rather than ways of engaging the learners' minds. They also left unchanged the basic agenda of 'science for scientists' rather than science for citizens.

Soon afterwards there was a concerted attempt to focus on science at work, in the home and the locality, and to plan activities which extend pupils from whatever level of skill and confidence they are already at. Present-day schemes offer much more varied activity sheets,[4] which provide structured guidance on such things as: keeping a systematic record of electricity meter readings when different devices are switched on, comparing the weather maps for several successive days, matching graphs to the written descriptions of them, collecting a range of vocabulary needed to distinguish different materials, and so on.[4] With such resources it is possible to set up a lively classroom, and if a pupil builds up a collection of them into a coherent record of personal work done, it represents a greater breadth of achievement than any of the older writing systems offered. It is however very easy for worksheets of any kind to be discarded after use and for the learner not to regard them as a valued possession.

Another danger with worksheets is that they can be received line by line, without requiring the pupil to work on the overall meaning of the topic at all. In an adolescent group where substantial attention is absorbed by urgent social concerns, a worksheet may get just enough attention to keep the task going, and no more. This is also true of some books when they do not belong to the pupils but are issued by teachers for work in class, with some instruction such as 'Read the section on page 25 and answer the questions about the diagram'. We can hardly claim in those circumstances that language is being used for the interpretation of meaning. Rather the writing is being done to avoid getting into trouble, to show that you have done some work, and to fill the time until the bell for the end of the lesson. To avoid that trap, both teacher and pupil have to have an eye on progress over weeks, and on what sense of achievement is going to come from the topic as a whole.

Many school syllabuses are now organised into short topics with that factor in mind – a positive sense of achievement, and clear gains made, within a period of only a few weeks. Logically, the end of the topic provides an ideal opportunity for the learners to sum up in their own words, but the ability to do that is itself something in which they have to be coached. We will have to be careful that self-assessments at the end of topics do not degrade into checklists offered by the teacher – a

form you have to fill up. Nevertheless, 'How well did I do?', 'What have I learned from this topic?' and 'What things did I find most difficult?' are useful prompts, and in principle there is a means here for developing a good dialogue on the progress of understanding.

Styles in what pupils read

Notwithstanding the administrative value in the modern classroom of having some well-designed activity sheets, there is also a case for more books, more continuous prose of all kinds, and particularly more in which the identity and personality of the writer is clear, so that it is easier to see the content as 'ideas expressed by so and so', rather than just 'facts you have to know'. It would make it so much clearer that the ideas of science are indeed made and remade by human beings, and cue readers into making sense of them anew.[5]

What makes anyone look seriously for the whole message in anything they hear or see or read, and attend to its meaning? Often it is some form of relationship with another person, some attention to the speaker, or in the case of a book an interest in the person behind what is on the page. Where there is such an interest or relationship the reading will involve a checking of ideas, but otherwise ideas easily degrade into information. That is why I proposed in Chapter 9 the idea of a 'story' or statement as the writing of a person, not just a disembodied piece of text.

Some very successful school text writers form a bond with their readers (the ones who do own the books, and who use them over and over again), simply by the excellence of their explanations. The reader comes to appreciate a manner of explanation which is recognisable from chapter to chapter. A few writers wear a more overt personality in their books; for example Keith Johnson in *Physics for You* (Hutchinson, 1978 and later). At the beginning of his GCSE version of this text he quotes Alice: **'What's the use of a book?' thought Alice, 'without pictures or conversations?'** He then makes sure that his pages are indeed enlivened by conversations, cartoons, and limericks or doggerel verses of the 'groan-groan' variety, which are nevertheless well integrated into the thought process of the topic. The reader can hardly be unaware of a person behind the words – someone exploring ideas, and inviting readers to do likewise. You cannot make the mistake of seeing the book simply as reported information. The example shown here is from the section on gas molecules and Brownian motion.

> A rather small student called Brown,
> Was asked why he danced up and down.
> He said 'Look you fools,
> It's the air molecules;
> They constantly knock me around!'

More groans are elicited by his table of 'Dotty Definitions':

- a painful measure of frequency?: hertz
- a quality of a wave which seems to be well and truly eaten?: amplitude

Johnson's is certainly a book which makes it easier for a teacher to pose the question: 'What do you think the author is trying to say?'

Although most school books are apparently addressed to the pupil, they set out a sequence of topics determined by a syllabus, not by the logic of communicating with a young reader, and so they are in some respects for the teacher, and not for the pupil at all. Often a page may be designed as a guide to a lesson and give instructions for activities – do this, try this . . . in a way which is really cueing the teacher on how to organise the lesson. Some school science books are an uncomfortable mixture of many things – part worksheet for bench science, part traditional text setting out the grammar of the subject, part illustrated magazine of the applications of science. Publishers have achieved very high standards of presentation, with these different components on the page, but it is open to question whether something for more continuous reading might not be a better provocation to thought.

In terms of the general ideas explored in this book it would be helpful to separate out two kinds of reading material corresponding to the two types of lesson mentioned earlier (p. 79):

(i) For lessons on exploring scientific ideas: short texts which are not obvious in their meaning, but need discussion

(ii) For learning the systematics of science: a text book nearer in style to those of some decades ago – key concepts, good summaries, and collections of problems

Material of the first kind must capture interest and if it can be mysterious, puzzling, enigmatic, teasing, so much the better. Many such items in our present composite books get passed over rather too quickly when they deserve more reflective thought, which they could get if they were specific objects of attention. (For example: just how small would the rather small student called Brown have to be?)

We also need more narrative that engages the reader, and books on scientific ideas which have an emotional appeal without sacrificing the need for good intellectual content. Books and classroom papers for an educational purpose do not have to ape the 'cold' style that is a feature of scientific description, and which is slightly exaggerated for effect in the following comment:

Talking of rainbows

Many men and women, since the waters of the deluge disappeared from the face of the earth, have looked at rainbows and have described them in many phrases, evoked by a sense of beauty and wonderment. These sensations are not noticeable when the physicist says 'the observer stands with his back to the sun, and all the raindrops at about 42° to the line joining the sun to his head appear red and those at about 40° appear violet. These form the primary bow. For the secondary bow the angular radius of the red is about 51° and of the blue about 54.5°.' No doubt this is an accurate statement of the principles underlying the formation of the rainbow, but it is hard to avoid the impression that something, something that appealed to Noah, is missing.

T. H. Savory (1953) in *The Language of Science*

Action points

I return now to the questions posed at the beginning of this chapter about fashions in working styles, and their purposes. In the design of rooms and in the kinds of writing which were required of pupils over many decades, we see the influence of a particular narrow range of objectives for science education. There have been many outward changes, but there is also a residual influence from earlier days and earlier ways which we should not be afraid to leave behind, in adapting to modern conditions and the wider range of objectives we now have.

A room set out for professional training is not the same as one arranged for exploring scientific ideas in the context of general education. To make science a study of people's meanings, and of the systems of talk and ways of seeing which science has developed, we should arrange rooms in ways consistent with that objective. That includes re-organising the space to allow for discussion, for presentations by pupils, for a better scrutiny of text rather than equipment, and for practical work which is connected with that scrutiny, and not just an end in itself.

The development of pupils' speech and writing as a means of understanding and coming to terms with scientific ideas has yet some way to go. Old styles in setting and marking work retain their influence. Newer roles for pupils as writers and speakers, and for teachers who can prepare them adequately for those roles, are developed only slowly, at the margins of a system still dominated by the expectation of practical work as the central feature.

In the resources used for science lessons we already have many guides to practical work, and many lavishly illustrated multi-purpose course books. On the other hand we have too few gripping narratives capable of grabbing and holding the reader's mind on a scientific topic, and too few materials of an enigmatic kind where the learner knows there is work to do, making sense of what is said. In the general style of a lesson it is the organisation of that work which is most central to the theme of this book. Words about science can not be taken for granted and thought of as some obvious commentary on experience, but should themselves be the focus of our attention, the object of a new kind of highly 'practical' word-work.

For the future we need an overall style of working in which the facilities, the written materials available for pupils, and the kinds of writing we get them to do all remind us that the meaning of scientific ideas is not something obvious, to be passed over ready-made, but that it requires interpretive effort.

Notes

1 The Wyggeston School chemistry laboratory, and other laboratories: An account of developments in Leicestershire was given by Malcolm Seaborne, in Brian Simon (ed.) (1968) *Education in Leicestershire 1540–1940*, Leicester University Press. The origins, purposes and effects of such laboratories are discussed by David Layton (1990) in 'Student laboratory practice and the history and philosophy of science', pp. 37–59 in Elizabeth Heggarty-Hazel (ed.) *The Student Laboratory and the Science Curriculum*, Routledge. See also Graeme Gooday (1990) 'Precision measurement and the genesis of physics teaching laboratories in Victorian Britain', *British Journal for the History of Science*, **23**, 25–51.

2 Traditions of writing in science: See (i) C. R. Sutton (1989) 'Writing and reading in science – the hidden messages' in Robin Millar (ed.) (1989) *Doing Science*, Falmer Press; (ii) Yanina Sheeran and Douglas Barnes (1991) *School Writing*, Open University Press, especially Chapter 2, 'Scientific writing'.

3 Variety of audience and variety of written task: *Twinned schools: The 'Science across Europe' Project*, co-ordinated by John Holman (ASE, Hatfield, 1991), has a unit of work in which pupils are encouraged to collect and organise information about the insulation systems in their own houses and then to send their account of it to pupils in a comparable school in another country.

Varied forms of writing: I am particularly grateful to Phil Findlay of Hinchinbrooke School, Huntingdon, for a great variety of pupils' scripts on many themes, from the serious to the splendidly trivial. The example of the diary of a charcoal burner arises from work done by teachers in South Wales and described to me by Colin Johnson.

4 Variety of task in the set worksheet or activity sheet: For examples for the early years of secondary schools, see Mike Coles, Richard Gott and Tony Thornley (1989) *Active Science*, Collins.

5 Styles in what pupils read: For an analysis of particular texts in terms of loss of a personal voice, and loss of expressions of doubt, see Paul Strube (1988) 'The presentation of energy and fields in physics texts – a case of literary inertia', *Physics Education*, **23**, 366–71. Only a part of what Strube is requesting in a 'considerate' book for learners is offered by Keith Johnson in *Physics for You*.

A NOTE TO THE READER

This last part of *Words, Science and Learning* is slightly more technical than earlier sections; you may need your pencil more often, to check and chart what I am saying and to compare it with your own thoughts! I want to discuss some of the words we use when we talk about the nature of science and those we use when we talk about learning and understanding.

For example, **discovery** has been an exciting word for children and others for several hundred years. How we feel about it could influence the way in which we try to find out about new things in our roles as learners, researchers or teachers. Like all words, however, it has not been entirely stable in its meanings, and to consider the changes it has suffered will help to illustrate further the view of language I have put forward in the main part of this book. It will also give a wider philosophical context within which to see the necessity of a re-appraisal of attitudes to language in school science.

Discovery meshes with **theory**, and with **fact** and with many other terms which I survey in Chapter 11, and then I turn in Chapter 12 to what we understand by **knowledge**, and consider the use of the idea of **constructivism** in relation to knowledge, and especially in relation to the understandings which particular learners have. Both these chapters were written immediately after the completion of Chapter 5, so they are in some respects an extension of the argument of that chapter.

'Discoveries', theories and 'facts'

However much we try to tie down the meanings of words in science, they still change over the years. That is true not only of words like **cell, element** and **acid**, but also of others like **observe, perceive** and **discover**, which might have been thought of as decently permanent without our help. Observing and perceiving were dealt with quite fully in Chapter 5, so I turn here to the word 'discover'.

Don't we all know what a scientific 'discovery' is? Isn't 'discovery' just a common sense idea – finding something or finding something out? Well, sadly we cannot take it for granted so easily today, and I explained in the notes to Chapter 2 how the word seems quaintly old fashioned when applied to ideas like 'latent heat' or 'specific heat' or the notion of a temperature scale, all of which have been carefully shaped by human beings.

Do we really 'dis-cover' anything, in the sense of just revealing to our awareness something which was there, fully formed, beforehand? Perhaps we do. Certainly I am very happy to **dis-cover** a missing bunch of keys when they have slipped under a cushion. I can also understand the claim that 'Captain Cook discovered Hawaii', notwithstanding the Eurocentric arrogance of such an expression (and other problems with it[1]). Overall, I accept such a phrasing because I believe that Captain Cook did find something, and at least he revealed it to European awareness. He did not *invent* the islands. However, others may later have invented 'Hawaii' as a political unit.

In much of science the situation is not like finding islands. It is much more difficult to say, for example, that J. J. Thomson 'discovered' electrons. We need something more like:

> The *idea* of electrons as negatively charged particles of fixed charge and mass was developed by the community of scientists, including especially Faraday, then Crookes, Thomson and others, and it was later changed considerably by Bohr, De Broglie, Schroedinger and Dirac.

Of course it is quicker, and convenient, to say that electrons have been discovered, but if we go on using the word 'discover' we shall need to accept that its meaning is not the simple common sense meaning.

Now that is just what happened to some of our most cherished words like 'fact' during the last 30 years. Observe, perceive and discover could not change alone without dragging **theory** and **fact** with them, and I want to outline the scope of the changes which these words have suffered.

Shifting meanings of 'theory' and 'fact'

The studies of perception outlined in Chapter 5 had effects not just on the philosophy of science but more generally on questions of epistemology – that is, they made more people think again about the grounds on which we may hold something to be firm knowledge. It became no longer possible to entertain a simple view that reliable knowledge is based on facts as the starting point, with theories built up later. Nor was it any longer possible to see observations and facts as nearly the same thing.

Gone was the idea of a simple progression:

sense data → percepts → concepts

Gone too was the Baconian recipe for getting firm knowledge:

facts → laws → theories of greater and greater explanatory power

Instead, a person's existing structure of ideas is now recognised as the starting point for knowing anything, and the act of theorising is seen to be part of the means of getting new understanding. Theories are understood as to some extent shaping the observed facts – both in what facts are to be regarded as significant, and what features of them are to be taken as most important.

I have tried to explore the new relationships in the adjacent diagram, and I start at the top with the word **theory**. Like most words, this has not had just one single and stable meaning. It began in Greek, in a family of words to do with looking upon, beholding, and being a spectator; hence it was used for the mental contemplations formed by the spectator. Over subsequent centuries it has come to be used in several different ways with its meaning shifting slightly according to context. We would not and should not expect that in 'theory of music' the word will mean exactly the same as in 'atomic theory'. All uses, however, include the idea of a **mental scheme** – sometimes highly speculative, sometimes much more firmly supported, sometimes explanatory, sometimes more like a set of rules for doing something (e.g. theory of government).

Scientists have given most attention to theory in the sense of an explanatory scheme such as the atomic theory, and they have not been content with explanation of what is already known, but keen to set up explanations which also have some predictive power. With this in mind, two ideas of what makes a good or poor theory have loomed large in scientific thought, and these are contrasted, in a slightly exaggerated way, in the upper section of the diagram:

(i) *Theory (1) (esteemed by scientists)* – is a well-articulated coherent system of ideas, accepted on the basis of well-understood evi-

dence, e.g. the ionic theory of electrolytes, the gene theory of inheritance.

(ii) *Theory (2) (excluded from science)* – refers to any powerful system of ideas which are not supported by public criteria to the same extent, e.g. theories of magic, astrology, etc.; some economic, political and educational theories.

Theory (1) has been valued in science because it connects with a system of clear hypotheses and testable predictions which enable us to design experiments. Sound scientific theories are felt to have a firmness about them because they have survived many tests by that checking route. By contrast, Theory (2) is easily belittled as just a **belief system** full of untested or untestable assumptions, and likely to generate 'opinions' of even less reliability. On the basis of this contrast it seemed possible to draw a clear line of demarcation between science and other areas of knowledge, as represented by the vertical line at the top of the diagram.

Theory (1) often relates closely with **model**. However, you might think that the word model implies more tentativeness (even in such long-established examples as the 'wave model' of light used to interpret optical interference and other optical phenomena). Perhaps it also suggests something which is less linguistic in character, more mathematical or visual, or perhaps nowadays based on sets of related suppositions interacting in a computer. Some commentators think of models as not linguistic at all, but that is not my view. I see all modelling as inspired by some associated imagery, which can in part be explored verbally. Models, like the metaphors on which I argue they are based, carry entailments or implications, and so they quickly yield the testable predictions which all scientists want.

In the middle decades of this century, these immediate connections of Theory (1), which are shown in the top central part of the diagram, seemed to capture key features of how science works, and many science teachers made use of them, stressing the provisional nature of scientific ideas, and the importance of experiment.

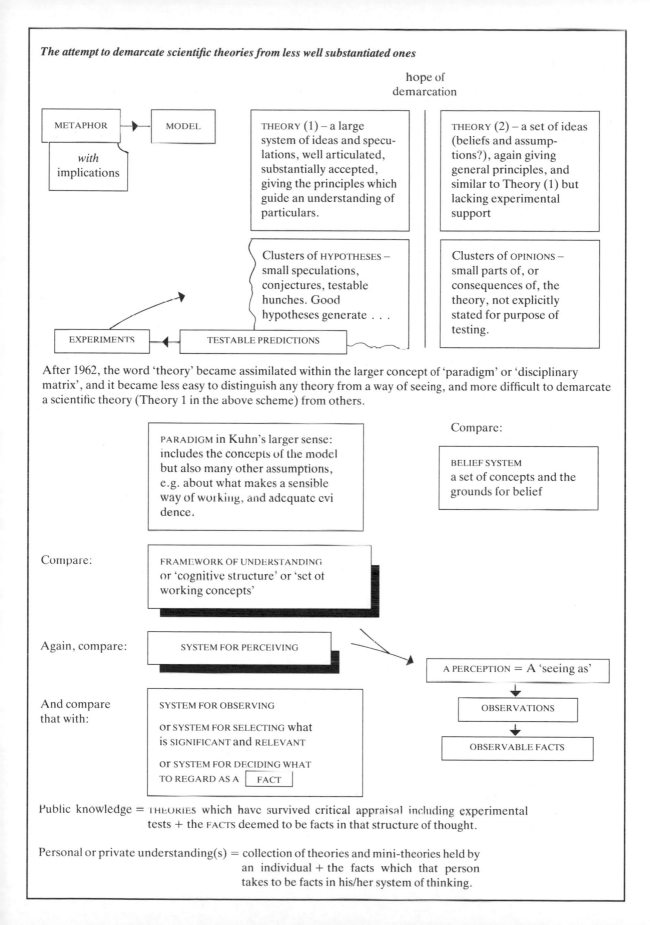

The attempt to demarcate scientific theories from less well substantiated ones

hope of
demarcation

METAPHOR ▸ MODEL

with
implications

THEORY (1) – a large
system of ideas and speculations, well articulated,
substantially accepted,
giving the principles which
guide an understanding of
particulars.

THEORY (2) – a set of ideas
(beliefs and assump-
tions?), again giving
general principles, and
similar to Theory (1) but
lacking experimental
support

Clusters of HYPOTHESES –
small speculations,
conjectures, testable
hunches. Good
hypotheses generate . . .

Clusters of OPINIONS –
small parts of, or
consequences of, the
theory, not explicitly
stated for purpose of
testing.

EXPERIMENTS ◂ TESTABLE PREDICTIONS

After 1962, the word 'theory' became assimilated within the larger concept of 'paradigm' or 'disciplinary
matrix', and it became less easy to distinguish any theory from a way of seeing, and more difficult to demarcate
a scientific theory (Theory 1 in the above scheme) from others.

Compare:

PARADIGM in Kuhn's larger sense:
includes the concepts of the model
but also many other assumptions,
e.g. about what makes a sensible
way of working, and adequate evi
dence.

BELIEF SYSTEM
a set of concepts and the
grounds for belief

Compare:

FRAMEWORK OF UNDERSTANDING
or 'cognitive structure' or 'set of
working concepts'

Again, compare:

SYSTEM FOR PERCEIVING

A PERCEPTION = A 'seeing as'

OBSERVATIONS

And compare
that with:

SYSTEM FOR OBSERVING

or SYSTEM FOR SELECTING what
is SIGNIFICANT and RELEVANT

or SYSTEM FOR DECIDING WHAT
TO REGARD AS A   FACT

OBSERVABLE FACTS

Public knowledge = THEORIES which have survived critical appraisal including experimental
tests + the FACTS deemed to be facts in that structure of thought.

Personal or private understanding(s) = collection of theories and mini-theories held by
an individual + the facts which that person
takes to be facts in his/her system of thinking.

Unfortunately, Theory (1) was meanwhile undergoing another transformation in which it became subsumed within a bigger idea. This transformation is strongly linked with the publication of *The Structure of Scientific Revolutions* by T. S. Kuhn in 1962. He brought to people's attention the idea that when anyone takes up a new theory they accept more than just the conceptual terms of the theory itself. Assumptions about good ways of working, about what would make a valid experimental test, and so on, are also taken on, and not all of these are explicit. Kuhn argued that these extra aspects were embodied in, and picked up from the 'paradigm cases' of highly admired investigations, such as Lavoisier's skilful use of weighing in connection with the oxygen theory of combustion. He took the word **paradigm** in that sense initially – and we could usefully make greater use of it in that primary sense of the great exemplar. However, as Kuhn wrote about the influence of such paradigm cases the word took on another and larger meaning – something more like a 'world-view', or as he later called it a 'disciplinary matrix'.

The advent of paradigm in the enlarged sense made it more difficult to maintain the demarcation between scientific theories and other belief systems, since the validity of the scientific test procedures is defined within the whole scheme of thought. Although what Kuhn called 'paradigm shift' involves communities and not just individuals, in its effects on individuals there are many similarities with 'Gestalt switch'. Taking up a new paradigm gives a new way of 'seeing as'. Studies of perception therefore lent support to Kuhn's historical and sociological studies, and helped to bring about acceptance of paradigm as a more inclusive term than theory, and one of great importance to an understanding of intellectual change.

Three decades later, paradigm in the larger sense (which Kuhn wanted to call the 'disciplinary matrix') almost equates with **framework of understanding** or 'cognitive structure' or 'set of working concepts', and this latter has come to be understood as a **system for perceiving**, which in turn is hardly different any longer from a **system for observing**. The human mind (or is it the brain?) is envisaged as having systems for selecting what to regard as significant or relevant, and *that* turns out to be in effect a means for deciding what shall be regarded as a **fact**!! The lower part of the diagram invites you to compare that flow of ideas. It shows facts as to some extent a product of thought, rather than its starting point.

Given this different approach to what a fact is, it is not surprising that Kuhn felt some satisfaction in assisting the republication of Ludwik Fleck's book from 1935 which had the rather startling title: *Genesis and Development of a Scientific Fact*.[2]

All this contrasts strongly with the very long-standing belief that the firm ground for our knowledge is observation of the facts of nature. In each generation since Francis Bacon's time at least lip service has been paid to that doctrine. For example, Darwin wrote in the preface to the *Origin of Species*:

> After five years' work I allowed myself to speculate . . .

He was expressing the accepted view that facts must come before theory, and recalling inaccurately the sequence of his own thought. It is refreshing to find that in a letter to a colleague he did also express something much nearer to the modern idea about theory and observation:

> About thirty years ago there was much talk that geologists ought only to observe and not theorise; and I well remember someone saying that at this rate a man might as well go into a gravel pit and count the pebbles and describe the colours. How odd it is that anyone should not see that all observation must be for or against some view if it is to be of any service.
>
> Charles Darwin: letter to Henry Fawcett, 18 September 1861 (quoted by Gillian Beer – see reference in the Notes to Chapter 3)

This musing by Darwin is atypical, and so pervasive has been the 'facts first' shibboleth that even the public understanding of forensic science has been contaminated by it: 'It is a capital mistake to theorise before one has data,' said Sherlock Holmes (for public consumption), yet all the while he had been listening for the dog that might have been expected to bark.

'Fact' and 'theory' in the classroom

School science has also been dominated by the data-first tradition, and indeed much of the recent debate about 'process science' occurred because new schemes of work were published which used an out-dated epistemology of that kind. However, it is not just the recent schemes. The notion of starting from the data is deeply ingrained in the language traditions of the science classroom, for example in how you write your 'conclusion', and in what you do *not* write before you go to the bench. I have described these traditions elsewhere in 'Writing and reading in science – the hidden messages'. (See reference in Note 2 of Chapter 10.) To turn this around will require not only a reappraisal of 'fact', 'theory', 'observe', 'perceive' and 'discover', but also the development of systems to help pupils write *more about ideas* and *less about practical work*.

To summarise what I have said about theory and fact, I can try to highlight three main stages of development for the usage of 'scientific theory':

(i) In the first stage, theories seem to arise from 'laws' which are simply generalisations from many individual facts which you can go out and 'discover', i.e. *new knowledge starts with facts* (Francis Bacon's idea).

(ii) In the second stage, theories are recognised as free creations of the human mind but you have to constrain them by checking. You can call them scientific if they generate hypotheses and hence experiments, so that they are in principle refutable, i.e. *You must check theories against the facts*. (This is a version of Karl Popper's hypothetico-deductive account of science, popular in the slightly over-simplified form which seemed to allow us to continue to regard 'the facts' as indisputable.)

(iii) In a further development that is still going on, theories are coming to be regarded as part of larger mental dispositions or thought systems, which shape our decisions about what to regard as factual, and the meanings of the words we use to describe it. From this point of view *facts come about by agreement while using a theory*. We use checking systems which include experiment but are not solely experimental (the Kuhnian stance).

School science still incorporates quite extensively the first and second of the above usages. Many lessons are Baconian, e.g. 'Heat these substances, see what happens, and then we'll find out if there are any patterns in the results'. Some lessons are more Popperian, e.g. 'What do you think would happen if . . .?' or 'How would you test that idea . . .?' It is difficult to do justice to the third approach without linking science into the history of ideas. It leads directly to lessons of the form: 'How did the idea of a "vitamin" arise, how does it connect with earlier and current ideas about food, what do we now mean by "vitamins" and what is the evidence for them?'

In Britain, the appearance in the national curriculum of a section called 'The Nature of Science' (Attainment Target 17 in the 1989 version) was not unconnected with the changes discussed here. Of course, it is not intended that the kind of 'philosophising' done in this chapter should be taught directly, or that we should engage pupils in arguments about 'scientific method'. The idea of a totally teachable correct method is one to avoid anyway because:

- There are important doubts about whether there is any such thing, in the sense of a reliable set of rules for making discoveries. (Hypothesis, criticism, experiment and publication are not readily encompassed neatly as a formula for success)
- In the context of professional preparation, scientists pick up their craft by apprenticeship and not by having it spelled out

What then can we do to communicate something of the nature of science[3] using ideas from this chapter? Perhaps the first thing is to stop using forms of speech from which a misleading impression is so easily picked up. For example, stop trying to force 'conclusions' as an apparent out-come from practical work, and stop speaking of facts as if there was no problem in deciding what is factual. More positively, we can emphasise the importance of *having ideas* and *testing ideas*. To show the tentativeness of theories we can use an 'as-if' phrasing, at least when introducing them for the first time: 'It is hard to know what "really" happens in this television tube but it is *as if* tiny charged particles were emitted from this part here. . . .' 'When we melt this piece of lead it is *as if* its tiniest pieces were able to roll over one another and fall away. . . .' And so on.[4]

We can show that ideas change over the years, and that they arise in response to particular problems at particular times in history. We can teach that science is a product of human beings. It is partly the false epistemology that scientific knowledge emerges from things rather than from breathing people that makes some adolescents reject science as not personally significant for them.[5]

Notes

1 Hawaii and 'discovery': Everyday meanings of the word 'discovery' have probably been influenced by the great 'Voyages of Discovery' such as those made by Captain Cook. To find an unsuspected island, or a new species of plant, or a new substance in chemistry, would all seem similar – mainly a matter of going out and looking. To find out that winds blow in interesting ways on either side of the equator, and to find out that birds migrate would also seem just a matter of going and looking. This may partly account for how we came to neglect the contribution made by the observer to an understanding of these relationships.

  Specifically in relation to the Hawaiian islands, the early settlers who peopled them are thought to have arrived from other parts of the Pacific in the fifth and tenth centuries AD. James Cook, arriving in 1778, called the islands the Sandwich Islands in deference to his First Lord of the Admiralty, the Earl of Sandwich, but as it turns out, that man's memory has been more permanently immortalised in the name of a humble snack of bread with filling.

2 Transgressing conventions in the use of the word 'fact': Ludwick Fleck wrote *Genesis and Development*

of a Scientific Fact in German in 1935. An English translation by Thaddeus Trenn was published 1978 by the University of Chicago Press, with a Foreword by T. S. Kuhn. 'How shocking' one might say; 'Surely a fact is a fact and not something that develops' – and Kuhn records just that reaction to the title. Fleck was a microbiologist, and his book was considered to be just a small part of the history of medicine until Kuhn publicised it as a more significant contribution to epistemology. It is interesting to see that such an analysis did come from inside the scientific community. In recent years it is sociologists who have written under titles calculated to have a similar shock-effect, e.g. K. D. Knorr-Cetina (1981) *The Manufacture of Knowledge*, Pergamon Press. See also Alan Chalmers (1990) *Science and its Fabrication*, Open University Press. It is interesting that 'manufacture' and 'fabrication' should seem somewhat offensive as applied to scientific knowledge, as in other contexts they represent positive achievements. Fleck's book has also been influential in spreading the notion that a 'thought collective' could be as important in science as in other areas of knowledge in supporting a way of seeing/way of talking/way of thinking. There was seen to be a social dimension to the formation of public knowledge.

3 Learning about the nature of science: What school learners pick up about science from their school experience is examined from several points of view in Robin Millar's book *Doing Science: Images of Science in Science Education*, Falmer Press, 1989. For recent disputes about 'process science' see Jerry Wellington (ed.) (1989) *Skills and Processes in Science Education – a critical analysis*, Routledge. Nicholas Selley's chapter in that book is one of several contributions to place these disputes in the wider context of how philosophy of science has or has not affected schools.

  For a more comprehensive survey of recent ideas on the nature of science see Alan Chalmers (1982) *What is this Thing called Science?* 2nd edn., Open University Press. For approaches to teaching about it in school, see Joan Solomon (ed.) (1989) *Teaching about the Nature of Science*, ASE, Hatfield.

4 The philosophy of 'as if': Hans Vaihinger wrote a book on this topic in the closing years of the last century: *The Philosophy of as if: a System of the Theoretical, Practical and Religious Fictions of Mankind*, English translation (1935) by C. K. Ogden, published by Kegan Paul, Trench and Trubner, London. The use of the 'as-if' phrasing was advocated to me most strongly by Frank Halliwell, organiser of

the Nuffield 'O'-Level chemistry project in the 1960s. If a teacher makes a point of speaking in this way when a particular theory is first introduced, the day-to-day usage in which theoretical entities are taken for granted seems less likely to mislead a learner? Compare Chapter 7 about language which is understood as having an interpretive function, and language which seems only to be a system of labelling.

5 The emotional appeal and personal significance of science: The emotional value of teaching science as a developing belief system was put very succinctly by John Colbeck (1978) in a letter to the *School Science Review*, **58**, 588. For a fuller treatment see John Head (1985) *The Personal Response to Science*, Cambridge University Press.

CHAPTER 12

Public knowledge and private understandings

In many parts of this book I have concentrated on what might be going on inside an individual's head, whether that individual be Torricelli starting to 'see' the ocean of air in 1643, or one of Arabella Buckley's children 'seeing' it a couple of centuries later in a personal version of the same insight (that example was discussed at the end of Chapter 5). Both science and education involve their participants in coming to see things in new ways, and in that respect – but only that – there is a good parallelism between scientist and child. They are both active in 'constructing' new ways to interpret the world in which they live.

Science, however, is not just concerned with the insights of individuals, and recent use of the word **constructivism** in the literature on children's learning in science has blurred an important distinction between individual insights and the product of collective activity by a community of scientists. Increasingly that latter is called **public knowledge**. I shall argue that we need to be more careful in distinguishing it from what is in any individual's mind, be that Scientist A, Scientist B or Child X. One way to do so with everyday words would be to make a point of speaking always of someone's **understanding** when you mean their individual ideas. I shall try to maintain that restraint at least in these immediate pages, using 'knowledge' for the public product, and 'understanding' for what an individual thinks (with 'understandings' in the plural to show the diversity).

Building public knowledge

T. S. Kuhn addressed the problem of how one person's new insight is transformed into publicly accepted knowledge in the scientific community.[1] He pointed out the social processes whereby the members of that community shift their agreed ways of understanding the topic. What begins as a Gestalt switch for the leading innovators continues as a more complex process in the network of researchers. The new view is scrutinised, tested, and accepted by some, who themselves undergo the switch. Gradually the community legitimises the new theory or refrains from doing so. If accepted, it gets enshrined in handbooks of research and then in textbooks of the subject. Some adherents of the old way of seeing may never change, and they are just left behind. A rising generation learns to talk in the new way, and quite apart from the legitimacy of the knowledge itself they gain the social advantages of speaking the language of their colleagues in the particular specialism.

Scrutiny of a new theory by a scientific community is a relatively formal process, and we can trace in it some separation in time between having ideas and weighing them up. I emphasise the separation in this two-component process to make it easier to comprehend what public knowledge is. If I divide the individual aspects of knowledge-making from its social aspects a bit too sharply,[2] I

Building public knowledge (a temporary structure of critically appraised theories with their 'facts' and defined terms)	=	Construction and reconstruction of personal understandings in the minds of individual scientists	+	An extended and relatively formal process of criticism, experiment, publication, and development of textbooks

find this at least a useful simplification on first acquaintance.

The phrase 'construction of public knowledge' would have a certain aptness to describe this communal effort, and we might say that the scientific community has laboured long and hard to construct the present edifice. Unfortunately as I have hinted already, the word 'construction' is being used mainly for what individuals do in their own minds, and so the longer process of insight plus legitimation will have to be distinguished in some other words. Let us just call it 'building' or **'building up' public knowledge**, with its two parts as above.

Public knowledge develops by using the insights of many contributing individuals, but is not identical with any of them. Books are important in maintaining it, but it is not exactly 'in' the books. The words, the marks on paper, form a starting point from which closely similar **understandings** can be re-created in the minds of individual readers, rather like closely similar cells can be re-created under the influence of a set of genes. We can perhaps say that public knowledge is the overlap in these many private understandings.

From a language point of view we should note the following features:

(i) Once a new area of such knowledge has been established, the textbooks present a series of carefully defined terms with a core of meaning that is specific to the topic. The small and inevitable variations in meaning from person to person that will still persist in the under-standings of individuals are played down. If an acid is to be defined as a proton donor, the other attributes which may be prominent in your thought about it are immediately ren-dered much less important than the core meaning.

(ii) The attention of the community becomes focused on those core meanings and the agreed public statements about them. We are confident of agreement, and in principle we could all repeat the supporting experiments. (More likely we are confident that someone else could do so!) We used to express that transferability by saying that science seeks knowledge which is 'objective' (i.e. not just one person's). Now we probably have to call it 'inter-subjective' or 'consensual', but it is certainly something shared, something sup-ported by groups of people who have access to the evidence.[1]

Building a new section of public knowledge therefore results in a certain intolerance of per-sonal variations of interpretation. For the practice of science one is not much concerned with people's individual mental versions of an idea, but more with what they have in common.

The concerns of a teacher

The first concern of a teacher, on the other hand, is with the ideas and understandings of individual learners, which are unlikely ever to be exactly the same for two people. For example, you and I may both understand acids in a modern way. We may have both developed some ideas about proton-donating behaviour, but the totality of your con-nections to this idea, or to acids generally, will not be quite the same as mine, and for each of us the further growth and development of meaning will depend on the details of those connections as well as on the core meaning.

To call these differing ideas of individuals **understandings** in the plural has several advantages. It emphasises the multiplicity of thought patterns, both within one person and from one to another, and invites us to explore and compare them. It is sufficiently wide in its application to include what people have tried to capture in phrases such as 'preconceptions', 'prior conceptions', 'alternative conceptions' and 'alternative frameworks', without demanding more precision than those terms have been able to sustain. Being an everyday word it does not imply any technical specialness, and it might help us to make more use of other common words like 'interpretation' and 'meaning'.

> Your *understanding* of the topic . . .
> Your *interpretation* of what is happening . . .
> The *meaning* as you understand it . . .

All these phrases give some status to the developing and changing thought patterns of an individual learner, without prejudice to further learning. Where emphasis is needed we can call them private understandings or personal understandings. They are after all, simply how a particular learner understands something. To firm up the key distinction all I have to do is to avoid the word 'knowledge' when referring to individuals. In school I can refer to the insights or understanding(s) of individual pupils, but not strictly to their knowledge! Mark you, that must apply to teachers too. I can claim understandings of my own, which hopefully include some areas of public knowledge, but I will have to make more conscious and deliberate use of phrases such as: 'I think the consensus about this topic is . . .' and 'My understanding has been . . .'

'Constructing' your own understanding

Researchers into children's learning in science have used the word 'construction' mainly about the internal processes in one person's mind: the sense making, interpretation or meaning-finding which is done by the active imagination of an individual thinker.

This is true even when Rosalind Driver[3] takes a general epistemological stance, writes about public knowledge, and considers children as constructing their own new understandings 'in a social context'. She is focusing on the construction of mental models *by individuals* – scientists or children. Her epistemology is a personal epistemology.

The popularity of 'constructivism' amongst researchers has come about despite some awkwardness in the history of the word. Expressions such as 'structures of thought' have been used for a long time, but recent uses of 'construct' in science education have been affected by two particular sources, one in *individual psychology*, the other from social psychology or *sociology*. The first, and more influential, is **Personal Construct Theory** as developed by George Kelly in the 1950s. The second is the **Social Construction of Knowledge** as outlined by Mead, Schutz, Berger, Luckmann and others. Having two such different sources has not helped to maintain consistency in what people understand by 'a constructivist perspective'.

Those who write about the social construction of knowledge are concerned not just with the formal processes of legitimation which I have already described. They have tried to trace a more intimate interaction when someone's social relationships are helping to shape their developing understanding. They might even question whether there is any such thing as developing a (verbal) understanding entirely on your own. That aspect is one to which Joan Solomon has drawn attention, as indicated already[2]. She argues that pupils in classrooms certainly do not make sense of things just by individual contemplation. Like any other human beings they try out their viewpoints and modes of talking with constant reference to other people who are emotionally significant to them. 'How do we know what we think?' involves, for them, both hearing what they find themselves saying, *and* feeling its connection with what other people say, so that they gain the assurance of a shared understanding.

Probably no one would doubt the importance of social interaction and a socially negotiated meaning when it is applied to things other than hard science. For example a teenager's beliefs about questions such as 'Is physics worth working at?' seem obviously socially negotiated. Joan Solomon's analysis suggests that we may have to consider it also in relation to the science itself, for example to that same teenager's beliefs about 'What does "work" mean?'

Constructing and construing

Most writers with a background in science teaching remain stubbornly psychological rather than sociological, and it is **personal constructs** that they have in mind, not **social constructs**. The central feature of Kelly's 'personal construct theory' should therefore be kept in mind. It is a two-fold process of what he called 'constructing' and 'construing':

Learners build mental models, and then . . .	These models become systems for interpreting new experience
(constructing)	*(construing)*

Mixing the metaphors somewhat, new mental furniture soon becomes a set of mental spectacles through which further experiences are seen, or the mental rooms we build for ourselves provide our only windows on the world. **Insights** about how the world works become **outlooks** for further interpretation of it.

What then can we say in summary about the use of the words 'construct', and 'construction' to describe how people form understandings? Despite the unfortunate blurring of the distinction between personal and social constructivism, this way of talking has stimulated much interest in pupils' understanding. It gets more people to laugh

---

> ### *Constructing and construing*
>
> Kelly used a pair of words to communicate the duality of interpretive mental activity. A human being **constructs** an understanding and then with its help **construes** or interprets further experience.
>
> To complicate the matter slightly he also used 'construct' as a noun. In his writings what the learner 'constructs' (verb) is referred to as a set of 'constructs' (noun)! and these then are the means of present and future construings!
>
> The intimate interweaving of these two elements can perhaps be felt in his otherwise confusing choice of words. Today the dominant meaning of 'to construe' is to do with interpreting, imputing, making sense of something, but that is a development of earlier meanings very close to the up-building idea of 'to construct'. Centuries ago, 'construe' was used to refer to building up a grammatical sentence, then to analysing one, and hence eventually it came to be associated with taking a sense or meaning from the sentence.

at the 'pot filling', 'empty vessel', *tabula rasa* or 'bucket' theories of the mind. It reminds us that the learner is an active agent with ideas of her own, and since she is also using these as 'mental spectacles' you had better listen pretty often to her description of what she sees. It also highlights a similarity between individual learners and individual scientists: both put on new spectacles as a result of their initial contemplations. Diagrammatically we can show the similarity (and its limits) as follows:

Learning science in school	=	**Construction and reconstruction of personal understandings in the minds of individual pupils** .	**in a social context of peers and teachers** (which is not an exact counterpart of the research community described earlier)

On the other hand:

Building public knowledge (a temporary structure of critically appraised theories with their 'facts' and defined terms)	=	Construction and reconstruction of personal understandings in the minds of individual scientists	+	An extended and relatively formal process of criticism, experiment, publication, and development of textbooks

Thought without feeling?

A more telling criticism of recent research on children's understanding in science is made by Guy Claxton.[3] He complains of the excessive concern of researchers with pupils' intellectual insights, as if teenagers were as cognitively tuned-in as the researchers themselves, and equally keen to sort out their understanding. He argues that 'Cognition doesn't matter if you're scared, depressed or bored' and that the constructivist perspective, as represented in current papers, has nothing to offer towards an understanding of the emotional response of learners. The question of how any topics and activities of school science may come to have real emotional significance to the learner remains to be addressed. (See also Note 5 at the end of Chapter 11.)

This neglect of feeling is slightly odd in view of the inspiration provided by George Kelly, because Kelly certainly included a person's interpretation of the emotional tone of things in what he meant by 'construing'. Perhaps investigators whose own background is in natural sciences have turned to cognitive psychology as nearer to the hard sciences. They may have esteemed it as a more likely source of insights on how to improve learning than anything to be found in the psychology of emotions or in books of sociology.

We should note also that 'construction' is a building metaphor which potentially excites implications to do with structures in two or three dimensions. 'Framework of understanding' points one's mind in a similar direction. It hints at the possibility of sketching how the parts are connected, drawing 'cognitive maps' to show the linkage of concepts and propositions within a structure. This line of thought has already been followed up by some researchers. Above all it suggests that the organisation of understanding *is* a structure and not, say, a soup with constantly shifting relationships. These ways of talking do clearly have some value, but they also have limitations, and the original metaphor should be kept under review. It may be guiding research in a way that misses key aspects of the learner's experience, such as her hopes and fears. Claxton suggests that maps of her cognitive understanding are not after all the most important thing.

New ways to talk about a learner's understanding-and-feeling together are perhaps the main priority for the future. If these are accompanied by changes in our beliefs about **public knowledge**, then it will be difficult not to adopt the negotiative style of interaction with pupils which is needed to help them explore the changing form of their own insights.

Notes

1 Use of 'objective', 'consensual', 'inter-subjective', etc. in relation to public knowledge: See John Ziman (1968) *Public Knowledge – the social dimension of science*, Cambridge University Press.

2 The social component in forming public knowledge: Some philosophers, and many sociologists of knowledge, have argued that there is a close interaction between the individual and the social aspects of knowing, as people negotiate what they feel they can together take as an adequate explanation. The concepts which emerge in shared knowledge are, on this account, *socially* constructed, because individuals require a sense of affirmation that other people who are emotionally significant to them share their way of understanding. Joan Solomon has discussed the application of this notion to classrooms, where relationships in the peer group, as well as with the teacher,

may shape what is negotiated, and the points of rest to which learners come in their development of understandings. See Joan Solomon (1987) 'Social influences on the construction of pupils' understanding of science', *Studies in Science Education*, **14**, 63–82.

A point which needs further consideration is how far the social process in the large scientific community differs from that in small groups such as a classroom. Is a scientist's participation in seminars and congresses, plus the custom of peer review of papers, plus the personal correspondence of scientists, just a slowed down version of the ordinary social negotiation which occurs in face to face interaction?

In the scientific community, scrutiny by peers is held to result eventually in the triumph of rational debate and detached weighing of evidence. Even when non-rational factors play a major part in the first reactions to a new theory, as for example in the initial hostility to the idea of continental drift, the scientific community holds that the gradual accumulation of more evidence, and the suggestion of conceivable mechanisms, was what led in the end to acceptance of that theory. Certainly the history of the topic can be read that way. Whatever it was that brought about the shift, people's unwillingness and inability to 'see' the continents moving was replaced by a positive engagement with the new imagery of tectonic plates and ocean-floor spreading.

3 The 'constructivist perspective' on knowledge and learning: For a concise summary of rationales underlying studies of children's understanding in science, which is written with a general epistemological stance in mind, see Rosalind Driver (1988) 'A constructivist approach to curriculum development' in Peter Fensham (ed.) *Development and Dilemmas in Science Education*, Falmer Press, and Rosalind Driver (1989) 'Changing conceptions' in Philip Adey (ed.) *Adolescent Development and School Science*, Falmer Press.

For an approach based more entirely in the psychology of young learners rather than in general epistemology, see Richard White (1988) *Learning Science*, Basil Blackwell. The most accessible general account of the topic is still Roger Osborne and Peter Freyberg's book (1985) *Learning in Science*, Heinemann.

For a full review of how considerations about the social construction of knowledge could impinge on science education see Joan Solomon (1987), *ibid.*, Note 2.

For the development of the idea of 'construing' using personal 'constructs' see George Kelly (1955) *The Psychology of Personal Constructs*, W. W. Norton & Co., New York.

For a criticism of the predominantly cognitive orientation of research on children's learning in science, see Guy Claxton (1989) 'Cognition doesn't matter if you're scared, depressed or bored' in Philip Adey (ed.) above, and Guy Claxton (1990) 'Science lessens?', an essay review in *Studies in Science Education*, **18**, 165–71. For a fuller consideration of the affective aspects of school science, see John Head (1985) *The Personal Response to Science*, Cambridge University Press.

Thanks

The stimulus to write this book has come from many people, but they are not responsible for any errors of logic or interpretation it may be felt to contain. Of those whose own thoughts have inspired or provoked the interpretation I now make I should particularly like to thank John Head, for a long insistence on a personal response to scientific ideas, John Haysom, Clive Carré, David Tawney, Joe Watson and other participants in the STEP work on science teacher training in the 1970s, and many colleagues at Leicester but especially John Baker, Jenny Harrison, Derek Holford, Laurence Rogers, David Tomley and Owen Watkins.

Without each other's knowledge, Peter Fensham and David Edge brought me into contact with key starting points that were otherwise remote from each other, and set in train the main themes about which I now write. Phil Findlay, Alan Jarvis, John Kramer, John Crookes, and many other teachers in Leicestershire or nearby have pushed me along the road of developing the present view from those starting points. So also have Hans Bouma and Ludo Brandt.

In putting the text together I have been greatly helped by my wife Carole, and other members of our family, and by Bill Brock, Duncan Cloud, Robin Millar, Keith Ross, Adrian Stokes, Joan Solomon and Martin Wenham, as well as by Brian Woolnough who crystallised the project, and John Skelton and staff of the Open University Press.

Afterword: How we talk about school learning

This book has been about language as an inter-pretive system in *the natural sciences*, and about pupils and teachers using it not only to make sense of their own experience, but also to enter imagin-atively into the ways of seeing and ways of talking which constitute modern science. Should we have a similar study of the language in which we interpret *education*? There are certainly many different ways of talking about it, and each system merits inspection, lest it be thought too easily that one particular way is the true, or only, way to understand what goes on in schools. People have made sense of the job in many different ways, and the competing systems of interpretation co-exist uneasily, or sometimes with obvious conflict about what constitutes a useful way to think about it. In this respect education is typical of the humanities; there is much less consensus about the most appropriate language than one finds in the natural sciences, possibly because it is more difficult to make an empirical check on the validity of any one system.

The method I have used in this book can be applied to any of these talk-systems and thought-systems which guide our actions in schools. We can try to make more explicit what the network is, how the chosen words connect, and what images link them. To do so might prevent us from assuming that one system is the only possible one, and when the dominant language forms are unhelpful, it might give us access to other interpretations. Conflicts about educational aims can often be

How shall we talk about education? *This little statue stands in the ancient university town of Leuven. Did the sculptor hope to warn us against a 'pot-filling' view of learning, or was he urging us to fill it well?*[1]

traced to different metaphors which the protagon-
ists are using to guide what they do, and several
studies have examined the language of education
in that way – looking for the metaphors which
inspire and guide different approaches to teaching.[2] Here are three of them:

● **Handing on ready-made knowledge?** Education is described in terms of giving and receiving information, 'passing on *knowledge*',
teaching the *content* of subjects, providing the
facts. This is close to the transmission view
described in Chapter 7. Even though it is often
lampooned as a 'pot-filling' view, its wide occur-
rence makes it at least a very important system
of talk.

● **Nurturing young minds?** More child-centred
teachers, who occasionally speak of themselves
as 'teachers of children, not subjects' are evidently guided by an image of education as a
process of 'nurture', assisting the 'growth' of the
learner. The associated language can even get
moderately horticultural if we talk about a
suitable 'climate' for learning and about the
'flowering' of young minds. Right-wing critics
reject it as an over-romantic conception of the
teacher's job, and vague about objectives. It is,
however, a way of talking which has inspired
many teachers.

● **Coaching in skills?** Another system, less
common in the traditional academic secondary
schools, but of increasing importance in the
general comprehensive secondary schools, cen-
tres around the idea of coaching pupils in *skills* –
life skills, subject-related skills and vocational
skills. It can be extended into rather precise
statements about what skills the learners are
expected to acquire. The teacher's role is seen as
that of manager and coach, helping learners to
reach gradually increasing levels of attainment,
or grades of skill. A current difficulty with this
way of talking is that written statements of
successive levels of attainment may be taken as a
prescription for an order of teaching, when
there is little evidence that they are sequentially
related. The image of 'ladders of success' may be
helpful in breaking down a complicated area

into small steps, but it easily implies one route
and one route only to the top of the ladder, and
reduces flexibility of approach for learner and
teacher.

The practice of secondary education is commonly influenced by a mixture of these three ways
of talking about it, even though individual teachers
may at various times conceive their personal
contribution more in terms of one view. In all
three, the initiative lies substantially with the
teacher (to present the subject, organise the
learning climate, or set out the skill targets). All
three tend to imply that the activities of education
are to be planned and organised by the teacher,
that things *begin* with teaching, and that the
learning follows afterwards – a view which can now
be questioned. They also accord considerable
professional autonomy to teachers, even though
other groups may be more distantly determining
what shall be taught. For example, in relation to
the idea of passing on a body of knowledge, the
political establishment, learned societies, universi-
ties and examination boards determine 'what
knowledge is of most worth', and they are therefore the Lords of the Curriculum whom teachers
serve, whilst nevertheless enjoying substantial
professional freedom of decision. In relation to the
third view, it can be held that employers, parents,
and in a more limited way the pupils themselves,
determine what skills are to be regarded as important.

Because of the high status of the teacher in these
long-established ways of talking it is worth examin-
ing here another system, which reduces the autonomy of the teacher quite markedly. This involves
the idea of **delivery** of the curriculum:

● **'Delivering' a curriculum?** Phrasing of this
kind is a product of the 1980s. Are we talking of
'delivery' as in 'missile delivery systems' one
wonders? Delivery has been associated with
nuclear weapons on the one hand and midwives
and babies on the other, as well as with post-
persons. Which way is the mind led by this new
phrasing? Those who brought it into discussions
of schooling probably took it from the world of
business – delivering, according to contract, the

goods or services promised – so its strongest connections are to 'contract' and 'promise', and 'accountability'.

The word curriculum (= a course to be run) has always implied some external prescription in the contract of what pupils are to be asked to learn, but 'delivery of the curriculum' takes a lot for granted about how its suitability can be specified in advance, and learning guaranteed. It seems also to deprive teachers of the responsibility for strategic and tactical planning, and it offers no decision-making role at all for the learners.[3]

Negotiation of learning plans, and negotiation of meanings?

All four of the ways of talking discussed so far take away responsibility and initiative from the learner. They do not suggest the planning of personal agendas in what is to be learned. They do not draw attention to what the learner already understands, nor do they suggest the process of construction and reconstruction of understanding by the learner which I described in Chapter 12. In this respect they are not well suited to the schools of the future, and certainly not for adult education and the 'life-long learning' which is projected as a feature of future society.

The most likely alternative talk-system which would give an appropriate change of emphasis is one using the word **negotiation**. It is already used by those who wish to maintain in adolescents a sense of personal control and responsibility for their own learning, and is associated with a teaching style which starts from records of progress, and encourages individuals to form action plans for the next stage in their learning, i.e. it is primarily negotiation of targets and schedules. In terms of the content of subjects, however, the view of meaning developed in this book makes **negotiation** an essential word to describe the extraction and re-creation of scientific meanings, with the learner having more responsibility for active sorting out and consultation about progress in understanding. Negotiation of meaning, interpretation of ideas, even 'decoding together the ideas which science has developed' are all possible descriptions of the core activity which I described in Chapter 9 – basing the science lesson on a close examination of a statement of scientific ideas. The lack of an established vocabulary for discussing learning and teaching in this way is just beginning to be overcome. I hope that this book will be a contribution to its development.

Notes

1 The fountain at Leuven: I am grateful to Dr Ludo Brandt for the following information about this figurine. It was erected in 1976 in the centre of Leuven and close to the university. The artist was Jef Claerhout. Its formal title was 'Fons Sapientiae – the Source of Wisdom'. The word 'Fons' is also a common Flemish forename, and the citizens and students of the town have named it 'Fonske', i.e. little Fons.

2 Root metaphors which inspire and guide educational practice: The topic is discussed extensively in (i) W. Taylor (ed.) (1984) *Metaphors of Education*, Heinemann, and (ii) I. Scheffler (1960) *The language of Education*, C. C. Thomas, Springfield, Illinois.

3 Metaphors about the curriculum: See (i) Denis Lawton (1984) 'Metaphors and the curriculum' in W. Taylor, *ibid.*; (ii) C. R. Sutton (1979) 'Talking about curriculum change', *Journal of Curriculum Studies*, **10**, 349–51.

Index

Index of some of the words discussed in this book

Index of some of the writers mentioned in this book